I0085234

She is Strong

Unleashing the Power of Your Design

FIONA PYSZKA

Published, April 2019
Fiona Inc.
www.fionainc.com
717-917-8101

Unless otherwise identified, Bible quotations in this book are from the Amplified, New Living Translation (NLT) and the King James versions of the Bible.

© 2019 by Fiona Inc.
All rights reserved. No part of this document may be reproduced or transmitted in any form or by any means, electronic, mechanical, photocopying, recording, or otherwise, without prior written permission of Fiona Inc. Copyright © 2019 FIONA PYSZKA

All rights reserved.

ISBN: 0-9993844-5-7
ISBN-13: 978-0-9993844-5-9

DEDICATION

I dedicate this book to my friends and family. To the amazing men and women in my life that have done exploits for the Kingdom of God. Especially my late parents, Rev. and Mrs. Surujpaul (1948-2018). I miss and love you both.

CONTENTS

ACKNOWLEDGMENTS

I am so grateful for the wonderful people that surround my life. My husband, children and family. I am thankful for those who graciously edit these pages to make them readable and usable for the masses. I would like to thank my wonderful parents who raised me to be a free thinking girl. It has turned me into a strong thinking woman today.

In Memory of my parents:

Rev. and Mrs. Surujpaul (1948-2018)

FOREWORD

Fiona Pyszka has a passion to help women find their place in society and in the Kingdom of God. Too many times women have felt like they are second rate and cower behind their husband or wonder where their place is and how they should walk out what they believe God has spoken to them. This book "She is Strong" will be a great blessing to all women but especially to women who are struggling to step into their rightful place in Christ. This book will help women to be free to pursue their calling in God.

This book will also be a tremendous help for men to encourage their wives and other women they know to follow their dreams. I come from a family of 7 boys and 5 girls. I have seen my sisters rise up to be the women of God they are destined to be. This book will help strong women help many other women to rise up and be strong. Fiona's heart to see women rise up in their callings and giftings comes through loud and clear in this book.

I recommend this book and believe it will be a great blessing to all who read it.

- Pastor Sam Smucker,
Regional Director RMAI

Let us talk about the lioness for a moment. The lioness is a graceful and beautiful creature. She is independent, yet she knows her place within the pride. She is protective and fierce regarding her cubs, yet loving and gentle in her care for them. She is a great and stealthy hunter providing food for her pride...and yes, even for her 'lion' to whom she is most loyal. She knows that her lion will protect her, and they will stand together to protect the pride. She even knows that, if the need arises, she can be as powerful as her lion. Her roar may not be as loud...but it is just as fierce and brave and strong.

Ladies, has your ROAR been muffled? Do you not know that Father God created you to not only be graceful, gentle, loyal and beautiful - but fierce, brave and STRONG?

The Proverbs 31 woman is not a woman who would shrink away from any adversity. She is a LIONESS providing for her family (even her maidservants). She is a wise woman who loves, provides, and protects in all loyalty.

I doubt there would have been songs written of Deborah, the great prophetess and judge of Israel, if she would have allowed her inner-roar to be stifled. Would all of the Jews in Persia have been murdered as a result of Haman's deceit if Esther had not stepped out in courage to plead before King Xerxes? Would King David have been born if Ruth had not been so loyal to Naomi?

The New Testament is also full of amazing lionesses. Mary, the obedient mother of Jesus; Mary Magdalene, whose loyalty lead to her being the first person to announce Jesus' resurrection; Susanna, who provided out of her resources for Jesus' ministry; Priscilla and Aquila who risked their own lives to save Paul…the list goes on and on and on.

I pray that you are a woman in search of your inner-lioness, and you are ready to release your roar as a warrior for the Kingdom of God, because you have definitely picked up the right book to begin the journey of discovering your destiny. Within the following pages of She is Strong, Fiona Pyszka will lead you to the truth about the God-given strength of women. She will bring to life the fact that it is the Lord's delight to release the lioness in all of His daughters. He longs to see all women walk in the fullness of their calling: courageous, confident, and strong in the power of His Spirit. You were made to stand alongside the lions in this world…to be partners and equal warriors for the Most-High God, the Lion of Judea.

Now…go find the strength in your ROAR!

Kristy Fricker
Senior Media Producer
Israel TV Network
Israeltvnetwork.tv

INTRODUCTION

Are you tired of feeling underestimated, suppressed, misjudged or frustrated?

You're not alone. If you've dreamed about being free to express who you really are, then this book will give you the roadmap to victory.

Come discover the true meaning of strength and how to properly unleash it.

No more fear. No more waiting. No more condemnation of not being good enough, strong enough or just . . . enough.

It's time to grab a hold of real truth to get real results.

SHE IS STRONG will get you there.

SHE IS STRONG

1 CREATED WITH STRENGTH

When you think of a strong woman what comes to mind? Do you think lace and a tea setting, stern faced and confrontational or decisive and influential? Your reflex answer to my question will give you a litmus test of where you stand on the subject of women and strength.

Do you think all women should be strong? Even more importantly, do you consider yourself to be a strong woman? Whether you believe women should be strong or not depends greatly on your definition of woman and your definition of strong.

Both words can bring about polarizing discussions and divisions in society. Popular culture today has secured many ways of displaying the strength of women. From the #metoo movement to mass marches, women are coming forward to announce their strength and their courage to not be made inferior or go unnoticed anymore.

In this book we will discuss the normalcy of women being strong. God did not create some women to be strong and others to be weak. He created a woman who was strong and capable of ruling and reigning in the Garden of Eden alongside her husband. The work necessary to be completed in Adam and Eve's environment before the fall did not require the sweat of the brow, it relied on the words of their mouth.

Whatever Adam named the animals and trees in the

Garden, that was their name.

> *Genesis 2:19-20 (NLT) - 19 So the Lord God formed from the ground all the wild animals and all the birds of the sky. He brought them to the man[a] to see what he would call them, and the man chose a name for each one. 20 He gave names to all the livestock, all the birds of the sky, and all the wild animals. But still there was no helper just right for him.*

This all happened before woman was ever created to help the man. Here is when God brought woman in:

> *Genesis 2:21-24 (NLT) - 21 So the Lord God caused the man to fall into a deep sleep. While the man slept, the Lord God took out one of the man's ribs and closed up the opening. 22 Then the Lord God made a woman from the rib, and he brought her to the man. 23 "At last!" the man exclaimed."This one is bone from my bone,   and flesh from my flesh! She will be called 'woman,'   because she was taken from 'man.'" 24 This explains why a man leaves his father and mother and is joined to his wife, and the two are united into one.*

Adam saw everything else that God created before woman and none of the animals or birds was a suitable helper for Adam. He did not connect with any of them and did not see how they could help him. After Adam's decision that none of these creatures were suitable for Him, God caused Adam to fall into a deep sleep. Here we see the first surgery ever done on the human body. This is how God created the first woman.

The rib that God took from Adam did not leave a void in Adam, it just provided the starter that God needed to create someone that Adam could identify with. Adam and Eve would now be from the same human DNA.

When God presented Eve to Adam, he called her woman. God didn't, Adam did because God had given him the responsibility to name everything that was created. Adam named woman and prophesied the order for how a man and woman should live together. He said in verse 24 that a man should leave his father and mother to be joined to his wife so that they could become one. He also spoke of mother and father even though neither Adam or Eve had mother and father. They only knew Father, God. But Adam knew the plan of God for the future because he was connected to God and had the creative life of God in Him. Adam was authorized to create systems on earth that would work to bring multiplication and a thriving relationship with God.

Adam did not consider himself greater than Eve, he considered her to be bone of his bone and flesh of his flesh. He saw her as equal to him as compared to the other creatures that were presented to him. None of them were suitable because not only were they not the same DNA, but they also did not think like he did. Eve thought like Adam and he saw her as one with him.

Adam and Eve together had complete authority and control of the Garden of Eden. They talked with God in the cool of the day together. God did not only talk to Adam He talked to Eve too because both were hiding when God came to talk to them after they sinned.

Genesis 3:8-9 (NLT) -8 When the cool evening breezes were blowing, the man[a] and his wife heard the Lord God walking about in the garden. So they hid from the Lord God among the trees. 9 Then the Lord God called to the man, "Where are you?"

As you read on in the exchange between God, Adam, Eve and the serpent, you can see where God did not only talk to Adam, He spoke directly to Eve. He had dialog with them in that they answered questions He asked. To the serpent he announced a sentence and a foretelling of its relationship with mankind.

To Adam and Eve He told them what would happen because of their sin, and He relocated them to a safer place. The place was safer because if He had left them in the Garden, they would have eaten from the tree of life and lived forever in a sinful state. God's instructions to them in the beginning did not prohibit them from eating from that tree. He only prohibited them from eating of the tree of the knowledge of good and evil.

Genesis 2:16-17 (NLT) - 16 But the Lord God warned him, "You may freely eat the fruit of every tree in the garden— 17 except the tree of the knowledge of good and evil. If you eat its fruit, you are sure to die."

God created order and functions in order. He did not want to take back any of His Word that He had given to Adam and Eve when He placed them in the Garden. He simply had to accommodate their new death existence. Spiritually, meaning their direct connection to God, they were severed from the life of God. Because of their sin they were now connected to the death of Satan. So, according to the verse in John 10:10, they were connected to the thief, instead of the life giver.

John 10:10 (NLT) - 10 The thief's purpose is to steal and kill and destroy. My purpose is to give them a rich and satisfying life.

As you can see from this verse, the very spirit of man became like that of God's adversary, Satan. Adam and Eve could not be trusted to obey any more instructions God would give them. This is why God had to place guards at the entrance of the Garden.

Genesis 3:24 (NLT) - 24 After sending them out, the Lord God stationed mighty cherubim to the east of the Garden of Eden. And he placed a flaming sword that flashed back and forth to guard the way to the tree of life.

Free Will

As a result of their sin, Adam and Eve lost dominion over the earth. However, they never lost their free will. This is key in understanding the issue of women feeling less equal than men in today's culture. Somehow there is a misunderstanding of this scripture that causes man to think that God gave him dominion over woman.

Genesis 3:16 (NLT) 16 Then he said to the woman,"I will sharpen the pain of your pregnancy, and in pain you will give birth. And you will desire to control your husband, but he will rule over you."

As you can see in this verse, the wife will desire to

control her husband but instead he will rule over her. This was God showing them how their new sinful nature will be responding to each other. He was not saying that this is how He was redesigning mankind to operate. Everything that happened to Adam and Eve after they sinned was a result of their sinful nature, not a design of God's plan for them. Before the fall Adam saw Eve as bone of his bone and flesh of his flesh. Now he will see her as someone to rule over. That's what sin does to the human spirit. It causes fear to control you and lead you to make choices to compete with and rule over fellow man.

Adam and Eve's dead spirit was causing them to operate in fear instead of faith. They developed a competitive attitude now instead of a complementary attitude towards each other. So, Eve wanted to control Adam but he would rule over her. That's the nature of the enemy, not the nature of God. When God rules, He operates in love because He is love. God still wanted to have a relationship with man, but man was ashamed from their nakedness in God's presence. So just like love would do, He created a cover up for man.

Genesis 3:21 (NLT) - 21 And the Lord God made clothing from animal skins for Adam and his wife

Even though Adam and Eve sinned and were fallen, they still multiplied and brought forth children to populate the earth. God had already blessed man to be able to do this.

Genesis 1:28 (NLT) - 28 Then God blessed them and said, "Be fruitful and multiply. Fill the earth and govern it. Reign over the fish in the sea, the birds in the sky, and all the animals that scurry along the ground."

You have to understand that the fall brought a great divide between God and man and it handed over dominion of the earth to Satan, but it could never mess with the position of man in the creation model. God made man in His own image and put man in a position above animals. This is why Adam and Eve could only multiply with each other and not with an animal after the fall. As a matter of fact, Adam recognized who Eve was in light of multiplication and named her Eve after the fall.

> *Genesis 3:20 (NLT) - 20 Then the man—Adam—*
> *named his wife Eve, because she would be the mother*
> *of all who live.*

After the fall Adam did not discard Eve and consider her unworthy of being his helper. He saw her as someone that was still necessary to fulfill the blessing command that was put on them at their creation.

The things that changed about man after the fall is: First, they lost their dominion over earth, they gave it over to Satan and he then became the god of this world.

> *2 Corinthians 4:4 (NLT) - 4 Satan, who is the god of*
> *this world, has blinded the minds of those who don't*
> *believe. They are unable to see the glorious light of the*
> *Good News. They don't understand this message*
> *about the glory of Christ, who is the exact likeness of*
> *God.*

Secondly, they lost their home and the perfection in which they lived. Thirdly, they lost their love nature and received a fear nature. (Genesis 3:10). Fourth, they lost their awe of each other and were now going to compete: Adam to rule over Eve and Eve wanting to control Adam.

What man did not lose was their design of male and female or their free will. Adam still remained a man and Eve still remained a woman. Both of them kept their free will to choose what they would like to do with their life. For Eve, we see this in the naming of their children. Eve named her sons. Adam did not scold her or exhibit his need to name the children. No, they both operated freely to do what was needed to be done to fulfill the multiplication mandate that was put on them.

> *Genesis 4:1-2 (NLT) - 4 Now Adam had sexual*
> *relations with his wife, Eve, and she became pregnant.*
> *When she gave birth to Cain, she said, "With the Lord's*
> *help, I have produced a man!" 2 Later she gave birth to*
> *his brother and named him Abel.*

With all that mankind lost, they did not lose the purpose of multiplication for which they were created.

Definition of a Strong Woman

With the understanding of what happened in creation and after the fall of man, this book will define a strong woman as a woman that uses her free will to follow the commands of God and bear fruit that honors His Kingdom.

Although Eve's spirit was dead and sinful, she still used her free will to accomplish what she could for God. Today, we have been given a second chance as the human race. God sent a ransom to purchase back our authority that was lost to Satan. He sent Jesus to be the payment to buy back what Satan stole. The pawn shop of hell required a payment for the release of human prisoners of death. Jesus came in place of us, before we ever got here and He made the payment. Now, both men and women can access the upgrade patch of redemption to be made new so that they can operate like Adam and Eve were originally created to operate.

> *Hebrews 9:15 (NLT) - 15 That is why he is the one who mediates a new covenant between God and people, so that all who are called can receive the eternal inheritance God has promised them. For Christ died to set them free from the penalty of the sins they had committed under that first covenant.*

A strong woman operates in this new freedom by accepting Jesus as her Savior from a sinful existence. She then uses her words in faith instead of fear to control her world. She does not control other people; she controls the atmosphere of the place that God has put her. She does not allow the enemy to talk her out of obedience to God; she sends the enemy away by submitting to God and resisting the devil (see James 4:7).

Two Systems

There are two belief systems that insinuate that women should be strong enough to not need a man and that men should be afraid of strong women. This is not true. Men, whether present or absent, do not make a woman strong. Both men and women need each other to properly serve the world with the giftings and abilities that they each posses. A woman's strength is developed individually and is her responsibility to foster so that she can be a pillar for the Kingdom of God, wherever in the world God sends her.

In our culture today, it seems that whether a woman should show strength or not is linked to her fall in the Garden of Eden. She is judged by the fall for leading her husband into sin. This makes her disqualified to be a leader and by effect must submit to being weaker than the men in the room. This is not true and it is the reason that the women of the world system have created movements to announce their womanhood.

In the Kingdom of Heaven women are recognized by God as equal in ability, calling and gifting to do what God created them to do. It is with this premise that I present to you the reason women must be strong. If we do not stand strong, then in the day of adversity we will fail.

Proverbs 24:10 (NLT) -If you fail under pressure, your strength is too small.

The enemy wants you to fail. That is his plan for your life. But God wants you to win over the enemy every time. That's the right plan for your life - winning. To win you must be strong.

All of mankind are expected to stand strong in the dominion God created them to have over the enemy and to not give him any place. It is when we take this position of standing strong as women that we will do things for God never before seen.

One of my favorite verses in the Bible is found in the book of Daniel.

Daniel 11:32 (KJV) And such as do wickedly against the covenant shall he corrupt by flatteries: but the people that do know their God shall be strong, and do exploits.

The latter part says that those who know their God will be strong and do exploits. This means that you can do things that no one else has ever heard of or seen. God put things in you that He wants to bring out through you in relationship with Him.

This is true for any people, male or female. The key to being strong is to know God. We don't know God by having a relationship through other people, we know God by having a relationship with Him ourselves. This is why Jesus came, to be the door that we enter through to have a personal relationship with God. If you don't develop this level of intimacy yourself, then you will not be able to be strong. Not being strong is against God's will for you. Yes, you read correctly! *It is against God's will for you to be a weak woman.* But, thank God for His Word and His relationship with us that makes us strong. Once you've hooked into strong, you can then do exploits. This is huge. Your relationship with God is key to being strong and doing great things for the Kingdom of God.

After all, isn't this why we were created? To have dominion (Gen 1:26) and to reflect the image and likeness of God. Look at what God has done in His creation of the earth and its inhabitants. It is unsurpassable and unshakable. God is the definition of strong and we were created in His image. WOW!

In the rest of this book, I will show you how a strong woman operates in her strength and I will show you what a weak woman looks like and how she behaves. The difference between a strong and a weak woman is not as obvious as some assume. You will see how culture and the traditions of men worldwide have marred the image God created women to be. But be assured, God has never altered the image of women. Yesterday, today and tomorrow women will still be made in the image of God.

Ladies, beyond a shadow of a doubt, you were created to be strong and not just any strong, God strong.

2 THE ATMOSPHERE OF A STRONG WOMAN

Have you ever walked into a room of fresh baked bread? The atmosphere smells delicious. You can taste what you haven't even bitten into. I remember as a little girl my mom would make homemade bread. We'd walk into the house after school and be engulfed in this warm feeling of comfort food. What a warm memory I have of those days. We would immediately take the fresh bread loaded with butter melting down our hands and devour every buttery soaked crumb, licking our fingers as we go for seconds. It made for the best after school welcome. I can still embrace the atmosphere even though it was years ago.

Atmospheres are experienced through our senses and stored in our emotions. The storing of atmospheres happen when there is an emotional element attached to it. For example, even as I mention the smell of freshly baked bread, I can see myself in that South American kitchen again. I see the apartment size stove still warm from the masterpiece my mom baked. She would smile as she watched us enjoy her creation in the kitchen. It's the same kitchen I learned to cook family recipes for my children. These are all positive memories from what I would consider to be a great, familial and nurturing atmosphere in my life.

But, I am not naive to think that everyone feels this way about their childhood memories. You may very well be a person that can remember more bad atmospheres than good. I assure you this is not the end of your story. Even though I would love to live my entire life in the many awesome, freshly-baked bread smelling experiences, I know that I had to move forward to develop and build upon this great start I had.

Independently, I had to make choices to capitalize on the great, positive experiences I had as a girl. I can also assure you that outside of my positive home atmosphere at that age, I had many peers who created a discriminatory atmosphere against me because of my gender and race. Those negative judgmental attitudes did not move me because I was confident that God loved me.

I chose not to dwell in an atmosphere of negativity, bullying, abuse or strife or I would have been weakened. You can choose to do the same about the memories of your life. There is a way that you can discontinue the feeling and influence of such places.

Ruth

In the book of Ruth we see the story of a woman who changed the atmosphere of her life. She was in a family where her father-in-law, brother-in-law and husband died, leaving her with a bitter mother-in-law. Her atmosphere went from life to death quickly. She was now left with two options, stay and die or leave and live. Ruth was decisive in her choice to leave a life of death behind for a future of life ahead.

Ruth 1:14-17 (NLT) - 14 And again they wept together, and Orpah kissed her mother-in-law good-bye. But Ruth clung tightly to Naomi. 15 "Look," Naomi said to her, "your sister-in-law has gone back to her people and to her gods. You should do the same."

16 But Ruth replied, "Don't ask me to leave you and turn back. Wherever you go, I will go; wherever you live, I will live. Your people will be my people, and your God will be my God. 17 Wherever you die, I will die,

and there I will be buried. May the Lord punish me
severely if I allow anything but death to separate us!"

I like Ruth's reply in verse 16. She put her foot down and said *don't ask me to turn back*. She was ready to move forward, she was ready to change the atmosphere of death and despair for a place where God had been good to the people. Her mother-in-law made a compelling argument for why Ruth should remain in Moab, and her sister-in-law made a bold move to walk away. Neither of them persuaded Ruth to change her mind. Ruth exhibited strength in a very tough environment.

There is a statement I use to describe someone who determines their outcome versus someone who reflects their circumstances. It is this, "Be a thermostat not a thermometer". A thermostat sets the temperature of the room, while a thermometer can merely reflect it. The thermometer is always at the mercy of the environment it is in, while the environment is always at the mercy of the temperature the thermostat sets.

A strong woman is the thermostat of the room she is given authority by God to govern. While a weak woman can only tell you what the environment is like that she is given to govern. Weak women always complain about things needing to change, but never change because they carry the mindset of a thermometer.

Whether you're married or single, you have been given assignments by God to accomplish in order to bring glory and honor to His Kingdom. Your ability to take your authority in these places of assignment is key to winning the victory or losing to your enemy.

The major tool that a strong woman uses when setting the temperature of her atmosphere is the Word of God, not the words of the environment she was sent to conquer for the Kingdom. She doesn't gossip, complain, give up or threaten to quit because she can't take it anymore. No, she speaks the Word of God where she is sent and she enforces it's fulfillment of her assignment by maintaining a spirit of love, power and a sound mind (see 2 Tim 1:7).

Orpah

Unlike Ruth, Orpah displayed the textbook description of a thermometer. She responded to her environment by doing what she was told to do. She "went-with-the-flow". She left because both Naomi and Ruth left Moab, but on the way there her mother-in-law changed. She changed from "Sure come with me" to "Wait a minute I think we need to rethink this."

> *Ruth 1:8-14 (NLT) - But on the way, Naomi said to her two daughters-in-law, "Go back to your mothers' homes. And may the Lord reward you for your kindness to your husbands and to me. 9 May the Lord bless you with the security of another marriage." Then she kissed them good-bye, and they all broke down and wept.*
>
> *10 "No," they said. "We want to go with you to your people."*
>
> *11 But Naomi replied, "Why should you go on with me? Can I still give birth to other sons who could grow up to be your husbands? 12 No, my daughters, return to your parents' homes, for I am too old to marry again. And even if it were possible, and I were to get married tonight and bear sons, then what? 13 Would you wait for them to grow up and refuse to marry someone else? No, of course not, my daughters! Things are far more bitter for me than for you, because the Lord himself has raised his fist against me."*
>
> *14 And again they wept together, and Orpah kissed her mother-in-law good-bye. But Ruth clung tightly to Naomi.*

Verse 14 shows us how Orpah changed courses after she heard the compelling argument from Naomi made of why she should not make the journey. On the other hand we see that Ruth kicked in her thermostat and said, *Oh no don't tell me to go back* (see vs 16).

We have no more information on what Orpah went on to do with her life in Moab. But we do know that Ruth went on to be a strong woman in her new country.

She got married and got herself put in the genealogy of Jesus (see Matt. 1) WOW! What a change of life. Her thermostat attitude catapulted her from mediocrity to excellence. She went from a dead place to one full of life and multiplication.

Ruth's famous line has been recited many times in songs, poems and plays throughout history:

> *Ruth 1:16-18 - "..... Wherever you go, I will go; wherever you live, I will live. Your people will be my people, and your God will be my God..."*

God's Word

God's Word is the guide that tells you what settings to use in order to change a room. The story of Ruth was put as an example for us to follow and learn from. No matter what you're dealing with today, God can help you be the strong woman He created you to be through His Word.

For example, if you are dealing with strife, you can pull out the Word of God and declare in the atmosphere this is what God's Word says and this is what will happen in this family, in this workplace, in this church from now on. Let's look at Proverbs:

> *Proverbs 13:10 (AMP) Through pride and presumption come nothing but strife, But [skillful and godly] wisdom is with those who welcome [well-advised] counsel.*

Using the verse in Proverbs you can declare the following concerning your atmosphere: "I am submitted to skillful and godly wisdom and I welcome well-advised counsel. I reject pride and presumption, it stays far from me". A strong woman speaks the Word of God and does not accept the status quo or what was in the past. She carries this atmosphere with her wherever she goes. When people meet her they sense the atmosphere of no strife, supernatural wisdom and wise counsel. People will adjust to these principles when they come into her presence. She holds onto the standard of who she is and does not bend for anyone. This means whether the person is friend or foe, she still keeps a no strife, godly wisdom environment.

God has not given anyone authority over the

atmosphere of your life, only you have this authority because of free will. Maybe this is the first time you've heard this truth. As we saw in Genesis 1:26 both men and women were created in God's image. God's image is not split. He doesn't have a stronger side and a weak side. God's image is strong all the way around. When God wants someone to do something big for Him, He looks for the person that can hook up to His atmosphere of strength using His message as a guide.

Today's culture wants to tell women to be the best thermometer you can be. It wants you to believe that you will be domineering and overpowering as a thermostat. Know your place, stay in your corner of the culture and don't ruffle feathers. This is the mindset of your enemy, ladies. God wants the women in His Kingdom to be strong and to do exploits. In order to do this you need to know God more than you know the men in your life and the society around you.

The atmosphere of your life must be hooked up to the Kingdom of light and you must be the thermostat that sets the tone of the environment wherever you go.

3 THE THOUGHTS OF A STRONG WOMAN

Every person is expected to control their thought life. It is the one area of your life that you have full control of even when you're a child. No one can control your mind but you.

Now, I'm sure you've heard of mind control techniques and cults that control people's minds. But all of those things are just persuasion techniques that initiate the conversation they want you to start thinking about. In order for your mind to actually change, you have to do the changing. You have to accept the information being fed to you as truth that you want to live by, you choose to make it become part of your being. No one can change your mind but you.

Women who are in controlling relationships or are chronic people-pleasers often feel trapped and believe they are without options. But the truth is they have options, more options than they realize. If they would just arrest the thoughts of their controller or their need to please others when it enters their mind, those thoughts would be shattered and not have its intended effect on their actions.

2 Corinthians 10:4-5 (KJV) -4 (For the weapons of our warfare are not carnal, but mighty through God to the pulling down of strong holds;) 5 Casting down imaginations, and every high thing that exalteth itself

against the knowledge of God, and bringing into
captivity every thought to the obedience of Christ;

Every person has the responsibility for their *own* thought life. Your thoughts have their own life. They have a lifestyle that is represented through you. Whatever choices you make, life or death, they are driven by a thought you believe or allow to stay with you.

Thoughts live in your mind and feed your brain instructions that run your life. They tell you what to do and how to do it. You could read the Bible from cover to cover 1,000 times and still have to control your thoughts in order to have success. If you take what you've read in the Bible and allow a thought of failure to stay in your mind, no matter what the Bible tells you about your success, you won't be able to believe it.

Dr. Caroline Leaf, a cognitive neuroscientist, in her online blog says this about our heart and mind:

> *Healthy thoughts are involved in proper communication*
> *between the heart mini-brain and the skull brain,*
> *leading to the promotion of well-being by the heart's*
> *orchestration of the whole body's electromagnetic*
> *rhythm and harmony. Good thoughts also enhance the*
> *vascular system, thus preventing hypertension. -*
> *https://drleaf.com/about/the-perfect-you/*

Our thoughts affect our entire body. A strong woman cannot have a successful life if her body is always breaking down. When someone else wants to control your life they have to weaken you inside and out. They have to make you believe that you are not worth being whole. They have to convince you that you need them in order to function.

As you can imagine, if you develop a dependency on someone to the point where you cannot make one decision without their input and approval, then you are not developing your strength as a woman, you are developing your dependency on someone else.

God never expected Adam and Eve to depend on each other in the Garden of Eden, He expected them to multiply with each other. This means each person working at their maximum ability to multiply. They were supposed to depend on His instructions on what to do. Their dominion was given to them by God and He asked them to take dominion.

Multiplication

The great misconception of history has been that the multiplication God spoke to Adam and Eve was referring to making babies alone. It is so ingrained in some cultures that those who are not mamas are looked down on and feel like failures themselves. This is so far from the truth considering where God spoke those words.

He spoke to them in an environment of seed producing plants and trees; animals reproducing after their own kind and the God Head (Father, Son, Holy Spirit) creating everything in the Garden that Adam and Eve saw.

God also expected Adam and Eve to multiply His work in the Garden.

Since they were both created equally in the image and likeness of God, they were equipped to create like God did. God even gave them the ability to create other humans. But that's not where it stopped, it was only the beginning. They were asked to tend to the Garden and the expectation was that they would fill the whole earth.

> Genesis 1:28 (NLT) - 28 Then God blessed them and said, "Be fruitful and multiply. Fill the earth and govern it. Reign over the fish in the sea, the birds in the sky, and all the animals that scurry along the ground."

What were they expected to fill the whole earth with? They were supposed to do what God did in the Garden - fill the earth with the trees and animals and govern them . When God set the Garden up He put that ability in Adam and Eve to create Gardens all over the earth.

The key I would like to point out here is that God did not ask them to rule over each other, but to rule over the animals and trees God created in the Garden.

Human domination is an appetite of Satan. He wanted Adam and Eve to start controlling each other like he wanted to control them (see Genesis 3:16). He deceived Eve in the Garden to give away her authority to rule the earth, having dominion where she was authorized by God to have dominion. And she gave it to him. Adam did also! Neither of them have an edge over the other because of who did it first, they both gave their individual dominion over the things God created for them to their enemy, Satan.

So when society says that a "strong woman" is a woman that causes a man to fall like Adam did, it is a lie. He fell by his own free will to choose to disobey God just like Eve did. Even if his choice was through Eve's influence, he still made the choice himself.

The proof is found in God's dealing with the sins of them both after their disobedience. They both had consequences. If only Adam or Eve bore the sole responsibility of the overall sin, then only one would have been considered sinful by God. (Genesis 3:8-19).

A strong woman knows her own strengths and weaknesses. She strengthens herself in the Lord, not with the strength of another person. Yes, we should be there to support each other in times of need, but our true strength to carry on and the ammunition by which we fight, should always be God's Word and power in us. The Bible tells us that when we are weak, He (God) is strong (2 Corinthians 12:9-10).

When you start seeing yourself in light of someone else, you diminish who you are and weaken your position in life. What happens to you if the person you rely on the most suddenly is no longer in your life? What would happen to you personally, spiritually, financially or socially? Would you be able to handle life or would you fall apart?

God is the constant source of strength and wisdom in a strong woman's thought life. Let's look at Mary, the mother of Jesus and see how strong her thought life had to be in order to carry the Word (Jesus) in her womb, and then deliver Him to the world.

Mary

Mary is known all over the world as the "virgin Mary". Automatically it gives off the context of a young girl. If we're not careful we can consider Mary's initial obedience to God's request for her to be the Mother of Jesus as one coming to an innocent girl who didn't know any better than to say "Yes" to God. But that's not the case from God's perspective. God compared Mary to all other women. Of all the women present in this time in history, God chose Mary to be the mother of His only begotten Son. She would have to accept an assignment from God she only read about while growing up. She had to go against the thoughts of a culture that was still waiting for the Messiah to come. Never would they consider that she would be favored above all women. Let's look at the encounter in Luke 1.

> *Luke 1:26-29 (AMPC) -26 . . .the angel Gabriel was sent from God to a town of Galilee named Nazareth,*
>
> *27 To a girl never having been married and a virgin engaged to be married to a man whose name was Joseph, a descendant of the house of David; and the virgin's name was Mary.*
>
> *28 And he came to her and said, Hail, O favored one [endued with grace]! The Lord is with you! Blessed (favored of God) are you before all other women!*
>
> *29 But when she saw him, she was greatly troubled and disturbed and confused at what he said and kept revolving in her mind what such a greeting might mean.*

Notice in verse 29 Mary's thoughts were going in a whirlwind. She was troubled, disturbed and confused at what the angel said. These thoughts kept revolving in her mind as she wondered what the angel would mean by such a greeting. But she did not let those thoughts stay in her mind, she took them captive. She looked beyond them and asked the right questions. She wanted to know how she could do what the angel said since she was a virgin and never knew a man (See Luke 1:34-35). The angel answered her by letting her know that it would be a work of Holy Spirit. Mary's response shows that she took care of her original thought process by her response to God's message to her.

Luke 1:38 (AMPC) - 38 Then Mary said, Behold, I am the handmaiden of the Lord; let it be done to me according to what you have said. And the angel left her.

Mary set the stage for who she was. She was not a basket case of confusing and stressful thoughts, she was the handmaiden of the Lord. Therefore, it was easy for her to receive and accept God's assignment to her. She did not wonder around praying and fasting to see if it was God's will for her to do what He was asking her to do. No! She knew it was right for her to do because God asked her to do it.

She demonstrated the qualities of a woman with a sound mind. The mind of a strong woman is sound. It operates by the leading and anointing of Holy Spirit. It is not wishy-washy or double-minded as James puts it (see James 1:8). Even though thoughts in themselves are not sinful, a sound mind will produce more stable thoughts than double minded ones. The more wrong types of thoughts you dwell on, the more thought life management you have to do.

A strong woman knows how to control her own mind quickly, using the Word of God as a guide.

Control Your Thought Life

Being strong is not a one time, heroic event. It is a lifestyle and part of your character as a strong woman. It is a developmental state. You go from glory to glory (see 2 Corin 3:18)) not victory to worry. Women who are dependent on someone else to fix them generally cannot stand up against the wicked thoughts plaguing their own minds. Thoughts of gossip, slander, worry, fear, death, offense, unforgiveness and such vile things, control their mind and eventually their life. Strong women know how to show these thoughts whose boss. They don't entertain them as guests at a tea party. They arrest them!

Strong women put these thoughts through the filter

embedded in their mindset that acknowledges that their relationship with God is pure and Holy. Anything God asks them to do, they know He's already seen them capable, that's why He asked.

Strong women make frequent arrests daily on their thought life and starts with a cleaned up mind for the next day.

Suppressing Truth vs Arresting Lies

Mary was a strong woman. She made the decision to carry Jesus as her baby without the consent of anyone significant in her life. God was not manipulating her when He sent Gabriel to talk to her. It was no coincidence that the angel appeared to her when she was alone. The decision to carry Jesus in her womb was not that of family consensus, it was of personal choice.

Joseph was never consulted in her decision even though they were betrothed (married, except for the marriage consummation). The Bible would have given us insight to her thoughts on this if she considered it because it showed us her thoughts when the angel first appeared to her (see Luke 1: 29). Her decision to say yes to God without the consultation of her husband did not make her a bad wife. It made her an obedient woman of God. She did it fearlessly and confidently. Not one moment was given to what could happen to her by culture, family or religion.

Put yourself in her shoes. What are you afraid of happening to you if you step out and make decisions that could free your life or the life of your children? What would have happened to Mary's life if she had been afraid of what society would have thought of her? We would have probably never heard of her. She would not have been written in the Bible as Jesus' mother. Is there something that God wants you to do that could be recorded in history for generations to come? What could future generations learn from your act of obedience to God?

A strong woman stands on her personal obedience to God and sees it through to birthing.

Mary had many people to consider in her decision to

carry baby Jesus, but she knew her relationship with God was rock solid. When God chose her, He told her that she was favored above all women. This did not inflate her with pride, it awakened her gratitude.

Gratitude

Gratitude to God reveals that your work for God was your choice and not a coercion of man.

> *Luke 1:46-48 (NLT) - 46 Mary responded, "Oh, how my soul praises the Lord. 47 How my spirit rejoices in God my Savior! 48 For he took notice of his lowly servant girl, and from now on all generations will call me blessed.*

Mary praised God for the opportunity to carry the Savior in her womb. She considered herself blessed. She didn't wonder why she was chosen for such a "big" job by God. She didn't ask about all the other women or why He couldn't have asked one of them to do this. None of these thoughts ran through her mind. She was grateful for this great assignment from God. She sang about it and rejoiced over it. She carried out her assignment with joy.

The thoughts of strong women are surrounded by joy. It's the joy of the Lord that gives us strength. Not the anointing on our gifts or our ability to do amazing feats, although this is good. It is the joy of the Lord that gives us strength.

> *Nehemiah 8:10 (NLT) - ". . . Don't be dejected and sad, for the joy of the Lord is your strength!"*

This verse in Nehemiah shows us just how much strength joy can produce. It was spoken at a time when the people were rebuilding the wall. They were being mocked by their enemy. They were under threat of attack. So, in order to get the job completed, they had a building tool in one hand and a weapon, ready to defend themselves, in another. It was through this time in their life that they were reminded that the joy of the Lord is their strength. God's joy is not a bearing up or putting up with rules and regulations. It is a defense for the most strength sapping times of our life.

When Jesus thought of the cross set before Him, He did not think of it in a sad way, He thought of it joyfully. That's where He got the strength to go through what He knew He had to endure in order to save the world from the slavery of Satan.

> *Hebrews 12:2 (NLT) - 2 We do this by keeping our eyes on Jesus, the champion who initiates and perfects our faith. Because of the joy[b] awaiting him, he endured the cross, disregarding its shame. Now he is seated in the place of honor beside God's throne.*

Mary's son, Jesus, grew up to be joyful like His mama. Jesus was not birthed in anxiousness and sorrow. He was carried in joy and anticipation.

Mary was a strong woman, not just a virgin girl. Her strong womanhood was highly favored above all other women.

She finished her assignment from God well. She delivered her assignment so the world could benefit from Him.

What has God asked you to do? He chose you for your assignment because He considers you a strong woman. Don't entertain the weak thoughts of Satan's interception. Drown them in gratefulness to God for choosing you and create an atmosphere of joy so that you can catapult your strength to go to the next level in Him.

4 THE HEART OF A STRONG WOMAN

The heart is an incredible organ. Your body cannot survive without it. Medically you can live with one lung, one kidney, missing parts of your liver and even shortened bowels. But you could never live without your heart.

God considers the heart a safe and valuable place and shows this through His Word to us. Here is what He says that He will do to our heart:

> *Hebrews 10:16 (NLT) - "This is the new covenant I will make with my people on that day, says the Lord: I will put my laws in their hearts, and I will write them on their minds."*

God will put His laws in your heart and He will write the laws He put in your heart directly into your mind. My goodness! Can you see the personal touch that God has given to each of us? He personally puts His laws in the safe and valuable place of the heart He created in us. Then, to make sure that we think correctly about what's in our heart, He makes a written record of what He stored in our heart in our mind.

In other words, He puts the inventory list in our mind of what He put in our heart. Every child of God has this privilege. Let this thought sink into your spirit for a moment. You have been deposited with God's new covenant information inside of you. No one could take it away from you. The only way this covenant will not work for you is if you refuse to accept and walk in it.

A strong woman walks fully in her God given covenant rights as they are revealed to her. She does not allow someone else to dictate which covenant belongs to her and which ones she's permitted to have. Strong women don't live by permission of man, they live by revelation of Holy Spirit.

John 16:13 (NLT) - 13 When the Spirit of truth comes, he will guide you into all truth. He will not speak on his own but will tell you what he has heard. He will tell you about the future.

Jesus was preaching while on earth that when Holy Spirit comes He will reveal things to us. Well, thank God we are living in a time where Holy Spirit has come (Acts 2) and He is present with us to reveal the truth of the covenant of God that has been deposited in our hearts. As women of God we should constantly tap into this source available to us. If we don't then the only alternative left for women on the face of the earth is what the devil has set up.

The Devil's Agenda for Women

In the world system, women have been fighting for decades to have equal rights to do the same things that men can do. They are fighting to get paid the same wages that men get paid for doing the same job, among other things. This is how the devil treats women. He makes them fight for what is already theirs. Imagine owning your own home and everyday in order to sleep in your bed, you have to fight with the bank that you've paid your mortgage that month and therefore qualify to sleep in your bed tonight? That sounds absurd right? Well, so is women trying to "fight for the right" to have something that God has already given you the right to have.

In the Kingdom of God, women are equal to men.

Galatians 3:28 (NLT) - 28 There is no longer Jew or
Gentile, slave or free, male and female. For you are all

28

one in Christ Jesus.

Christian women should not have to bow to men. She does not have to defer important decisions and hard questions to men. No, she has been created equal in the eyes of God and counted as capable of utilizing the wisdom of God made available to all believers. A woman does not have missing brain cells or weaker spiritual vessels than men. Women were created by God in His image for His purpose. This will never change.

But if your heart can be changed into always defending your position, fighting for your rights and proving yourself instead of being the woman God created you to be, you will become Satan's mouthpiece to bring division among genders.

Satan wants to have war happening every day, everywhere and in every walk of life. He wants it between parents and children, races of people and genders. He wants to keep the ball of confusion spinning so that people will always feel out of control and one step away from losing it.

You are a woman of God and have a heart that will not operate in fear. You will not be one of the casualties of the last days where people's hearts will fail them for fear (Luke 21:26). You heart is set on God and that's what will keep you focused on what He's called you to do.

Heart and Peace

What should you do with your heart to continue as a strong woman? The Bible tells us the setting that we should put our heart in. Remember the analogy of the thermostat and the thermometer in Chapter 2? Your heart was created to operate at its optimum level by having certain settings. God has predesigned frequencies that He wants you to keep your heart tuned to, let's look at this scripture.

> *Colossians 3:15-16 (NLT) - 15 And let the peace that comes from Christ rule in your hearts. For as members of one body you are called to live in peace. And always be thankful. 16 Let the message about Christ, in all its*

*richness, fill your lives. Teach and counsel each other
with all the wisdom he gives. Sing psalms and hymns
and spiritual songs to God with thankful hearts.*

From just these two scriptures we see several settings for the heart that will cause us to live well with each other and to grow personally.

First, the peace of God is to be the ruler of the heart. This is a big task and a big decision we have to make. Do you want peace to rule or do you want fear to rule? This is a personal decision and we need to make the choice, God will never make it for us. He simply offers it and arranges its operation once we choose it.

Secondly, accept that you are an equal member of the body of Christ. You are not the underling or the lesser part, you are an equal member and you are called to live as one whole unit, not men and women. The world system is set up to live as men and women. This is Satan's design. God's design is shown in how Jesus and the apostles operated in the New Testament church. They utilized the gifts and abilities of believers. They did not use people for their "roles" in society. Men were chosen to wait on tables and serve widows food. Women were given the message of the resurrection to take to the men mourning the loss of Jesus. These were all done with the Spirit of one body living in unity for Jesus.

Thirdly, to be thankful for who God created you to be and not who you wish you could be. The devil has a very sound track record of causing people to wish they were someone else. Wishing being the operative word here. I don't like to use the word wish as it insinuates a magical spell of some sort, but in this case it is fitting as people really do want to magically be someone they are not. What is so wrong with being who you were created to be, except to be made to think that who you are is not good enough for where you are. The only person that would make such a ludicrous accusation towards you would be the devil. His kingdom hates who you are and wants to twist every part of you to distort the image of Christ in you. But, thankfulness for who you are will change all of that in a moment. Imagine a day where you go through life thanking

God for who you are and what you are able to do. Have you ever had such a day? Now is a good time to start that. Thank God for how He created you to operate, thank Him for how you do things that no one else is capable of doing like you do. Thank God for something. Let it come from your heart. It's stored in there, get it out with your mouth.

Lastly, wisdom should be what comes out of your mouth, not complaining layered with strife, gossip and disrespect. Let wisdom prevail in every situation of your life. This is a matter of the heart more than it is of the mind. The Bible tells us that wisdom is the principle thing (Proverbs 4:7). It tells us that with all we're going to get, make sure that we get understanding with our wisdom. If you don't understand what you have, then you won't know how to use it. Many people have the answers to their problems deposited already by God in their heart, but they do not know how to access it. Wisdom will help you do that. You have to walk in wisdom or you will walk in defeat.

Guard Your Heart

This is a critical security element you need to have in your life. If you don't guard your heart, then the thief can enter and steal what God has so graciously deposited in you. He can also plant things in your heart that does not belong to you or will corrupt you. God told us to guard our heart above everything else we guard.

Proverbs 4:23 (NLT) -23 Guard your heart above all else,   for it determines the course of your life.

In a bank there is a vault that is fixed with security safeguards. Why? Because it's where the money, the main product of a bank, is kept. You will not find the vault of a bank in the lobby of the bank wide open for anyone to walk into. This would be the most foolish bank in existence and I would never put my money there. It's the same way with your heart. You must have it safely tucked behind security system measures that warn you when danger is near. I'm sure there are intricate details that surround vault's security system that is not visible to the general public. Same with your heart. You need to put things in place that will alert you when someone is trying to get into your heart illegally.

What does this look like? The words of the person do not match the words of your Creator. If Eve was doing this guarding of her heart, she should have never answered the enemy the way she did. The only words that she would have had to answer him with would have been, "Get thee behind me Satan" because we see that's how Jesus answered His temptation when He was getting ready to fulfill His purpose.

Matthew 16:23 (NLT) - 23 Jesus turned to Peter and said, "Get away from me, Satan! You are a dangerous trap to me. You are seeing things merely from a human point of view, not from God's."

Jesus did not have deposited in Him a desire to disobey God's plan for His life, instead He had the joy set before Him to endure the cross (see Hebrews 12:2). He was willing to guard that plan. The words He said to Peter were directed at the enemy that was working through Peter disguised as concern and a desire for Jesus to not be harmed. But in fact, Jesus was supposed to die and be very much harmed if He was to fulfill the purpose for which He came. He could not be the Savior of the world if He did not go to the cross and raise again on the third day. All of this was being discussed when Peter said *No, this shall not happen to you.* If Jesus would have agreed with Peter's version of what should happen in His life, then Jesus would have disobeyed God's plan for His life. This would have been rebellion and Jesus would have forfeited the reason for His arrival on earth. Do you see the trap and the downward spiraling effect that could occur from an unguarded heart?

It is critical to your life and well being that you guard your heart with ALL diligence. Out of it flows the issues of your life. Good issues and bad issues. All flow from what type of guard system you have built for your heart.

Your Voice

You will not be able to speak truthfully about something that you do not believe in your heart. When you first receive salvation you have to believe in your heart before you confess with your mouth. If you don't believe in your heart, then confession out of the mouth is not true for you. You may be saying something that is in the Bible that is Truth, but for you it may not be true, because it is not believed in your heart.

> *Romans 10:9 (NLT) - 9 If you openly declare that*
> *Jesus is Lord and believe in your heart that God raised*
> *him from the dead, you will be saved.*

The Bible gives us a great example of such a situation. It refers to a person who invites you in for a meal and encourages you to drink and eat, but in their hearts they're thinking about how much it's costing them. Their words are deceiving you to think that they are generous, but in their heart greed is stored.

> *Proverbs 23:7 (AMP)7 For as he thinks in his heart, so*
> *is he [in behavior—one who manipulates]. He says to*
> *you, "Eat and drink," Yet his heart is not with you [but*
> *it is begrudging the cost].*

God did not put greed in our hearts. When He wrote words on our mind, they were not words of greed or fear. Greed is a fruit of fear because there is a thought of lack. It causes you to keep tabs on how much you've given to someone, instead of giving like God did. God freely gave us all things to enjoy. This of course, does not mean that we let people stomp all over us and take advantage of things that we have been blessed with.

With the picture of how God offers His blessings to you, we have to also consider how we offer blessings to the world around us. Our voice gets messages from what we believe in our heart. If you say something that is not in your heart, then you are being deceitful. This is what Satan does. He hides the true reason why he says anything. He never speaks the truth. He always speaks lies.

If you say something that is not in your heart, you are lying. You're lying not only to the people you speak to, but most of all to yourself.

Don't confuse the use of faith filled words with reality words. Faith filled words come from having God's Word about a matter deposited in your heart. You then proceed to speak the outcome you expect to happen because of your belief in those words. Whereas, reality words are describing what you see on the outside, or your circumstances.

Your circumstances don't have to get into your heart. This is where guarding it comes into play. When you guard your heart properly, you will reject the circumstances surrounding you from infiltrating the Word of God that has been established in you. If you don't do this, then the circumstantial words, or the "what if" words will want to override the Word of God in your heart to bring confusion instead of solutions to the problems you face. What does this mean? Your voice is the container that dips into the heart and pours it through your mouth to give voice to the authority of God inside of you. It is also what you use to pray to God and agree with what He's put in you. If your heart gets corrupted by the circumstantial evidence of the world, then the pure Word of God in you will be held in question by the circumstantial evidence around you that you are focusing on. You will start to compare what God says to what you see. When this comparison happens, your mouth will want to accept the circumstances around you instead of God's pure words that are planted in your heart. This is what happened in the book of Acts.

Ananias Sapphira

There is a woman in the Bible who did not keep her heart guarded. She went along with the deception of her husband and ended up causing death to her family. Her name was Sapphira. Her and her husband Ananias were part of the church in the book of Acts. They were part of the revival that was happening after Holy Spirit fell on the 120 in the upper room. They were in the fresh move of God and seeing all of the miracles and generosity happening in their local church. They wanted to be recognized like the other givers who were selling their lands and houses and bringing the entire amount into the church to benefit the whole body. The only problem was that the substance in their heart was not generosity, it was greed. They were more interested in how they would look to others than how they would respect God with their giving. Their hearts were polluted by the deception of "appearing" good. Here's how Acts puts it.

Acts 5:1-2 (NLT) But there was a certain man named Ananias who, with his wife, Sapphira, sold some property. 2 He brought part of the money to the apostles, claiming it was the full amount. With his wife's consent, he kept the rest. 3 Then Peter said, "Ananias, why have you let Satan fill your heart? You lied to the Holy Spirit, and you kept some of the money for yourself.

So, they went through the motion of selling property and coming to church and giving an offering. The difference was their giving was a lie. Their heart of giving was filled with lies. Sounds like someone else we know from John 10:10, doesn't it? The thief that comes to steal, kill and destroy. They turned into the lie they believed in their heart. They both died. They refused to give up their new friend "lie" for their God given gift of Truth deposited in them.

Acts 5:5-10 New Living Translation (NLT) - As soon as Ananias heard these words, he fell to the floor and died. Everyone who heard about it was terrified. 6 Then some young men got up, wrapped him in a sheet, and took him out and buried him.

7 About three hours later his wife came in, not knowing what had happened. 8 Peter asked her, "Was this the price you and your husband received for your land?" "Yes," she replied, "that was the price." 9 And Peter said, "How could the two of you even think of conspiring to test the Spirit of the Lord like this? The young men who buried your husband are just outside the door, and they will carry you out, too." 10 Instantly, she fell to the floor and died. When the young men came in and saw that she was dead, they carried her out and buried her beside her husband.

Here we see a perfect example of a weak woman. She did not have a direct relationship with God to allow her to stand up in a plot of lies and say "No" to the lie. God gave her a chance in the presence of Holy Spirit, in God's own house and she still agreed with the standard of her lying heart. A strong woman would never compromise in this way. She would always keep her connection to God clean and clear. She would obey God above everyone else, even a husband. Yes I said it!

Unfortunately in society, even in some church cultures, it seems a taboo thing for a woman to go against the words or belief of her husband. She is considered to not be a "submitted" wife if she dares to go against his grain. Well, a submitted wife must first be submitted to God so that she has a gauge for what God intends for her to help her husband in. If her husband disrespects the authority of God and His house, then the wife has every right in the eyes of God to destroy those words from entering her heart. The way the Kingdom of God works is a strong woman can destroy the work of the enemy like Jesus did and told us to do.

> *1 John 3:8 (NLT) - 8 But when people keep on sinning, it shows that they belong to the devil, who has been sinning since the beginning. But the Son of God came to destroy the works of the devil.*

What I'm saying to you is so unpopular in today's culture that I'm liable to get stoned for even saying it. But it has to be said. Women have been bound too long by the slavery of the traditions of men. They have been held captive to the destructive systems of evil causing them to bypass the integrity of the Word of God in their heart for the doctrines of devils.

Authority

We are all subject to authority, men and women alike. That order has been established by God. He designed us to submit to Him as the ultimate authority. This means His Word is above every other word. No other human has been given permission by God to override another human's will. No one. Even God Himself will not do it. There is a misconception about God's authority when it comes to our life. This misconception has given people the idea that if God wanted something to happen for them, or in a certain situation, He would just make it happen. Well, that's not entirely true. God does not override our will to make something happen that we have decided we do not want to happen. If God did this, He would be no better than Satan. He would violate His own order of free will to mankind.

In the story of Adam and Eve, if God overrode wills as His standard operating procedure, He would have stopped Eve from interacting with Satan through the serpent. He would have caused every fruit from the tree that Eve was going to eat to fall to the ground and move away before she could eat it. He could have also sent her husband Adam running into her presence, guns blazing, to stop her in her actions to eat the fruit. But instead, He did no such thing. He left them to operate their own free will with His instructions already deposited in their hearts.

Every person has complete authority over what happens in their life. In the case of children, they are under the training of their parents, but they still have a will of their own. As parents, we should try our very best to respect the will of our children. Disciplining them only when their will rebels against God's laws not our made up preferences. Having a guideline and standard of how your house runs is great, and for every house it will look differently. However, the main issue needs to be that kids are not controlled but truly trained in how to use their wills to obey God's will.

Letting someone's voice be their authority over their own life can be one of the most difficult things to do, but it is biblical. We will all reap the fruit of our lips.

Proverbs 1:31 (NKJV) -31 Therefore they shall eat the fruit of their own way, And be filled to the full with their own fancies.

The Bible tells us also that wisdom will cry out to us, but if we keep rejecting God's wisdom to us, then we will reap the fruit of our own lips. Our voice is the authority of life or death in our life. God gave us this power. We are to use it of our own free will and do not allow someone else to "make" us do anything. Someone may be made to do something outwardly, but their heart thinks differently than what they are made to do, this is called deception. It doesn't matter if you're doing it because you're being held at gun point or if you're doing it because you're malicious and want to hurt someone, you are still involved in a plot of deception. It is the enemy's plot. The great news is that we have power over the works of the enemy. We can say with our mouths, *I take authority over the plans of the enemy right now and take my authority in Jesus Name that this work of the enemy must stop now.*

Every woman I know that has come out of a controlling relationship, has had to do some variation of this action of taking authority over the works of the enemy. If they didn't, they would have never been able to leave their controlling relationship.

The heart of a strong woman keeps the Word of God safe and actively uses it against the deception of the enemy. She conducts herself like Jesus did when He overcame the temptation of Satan in the wilderness. Jesus answered the enemy's deception with, "It is written". You can say that too, because the Word of God has been written in you.

5 THE LIFE OF A STRONG WOMAN

The life of a strong woman is first pleasing to God, then secondly pleasing to herself. She pleases God by serving Him with every part of her. Spirit, soul and body, nothing held back. She is not working on a part of her in secret so she could present it perfect to God. No! A strong woman puts it all on the line in front of God so He can have a say in her perfection. God is her Creator and she recognizes and acknowledges this truth. Her strength is not derived by how much she can handle before she breaks. Her strength is derived on her continual standing on God's Word. She builds herself up in the Word of God, then she fights from that position. She is pleasing to God because she believes everything He says. She knows that her strength is not what holds her up, but that it's God's Word as her foundation that does.

A strong woman is not looking for the approval of anyone around her before following instructions from God. She is pleased to serve God even in the midst of disapproving comments, stares or repercussions. Society is not the audience she stands strong for, God is.

A strong woman is very pleased with herself and how she is living life because she has put God first. The world system has defined a strong woman to be a woman that is completely independent. She is independent of God and of any wise counsel. This is not God's view of anyone that is strong, it is the position of a fool. The Bible tells us about the difference between a wise person and a fool.

Proverbs 15:12 (NLT) - 12 Mockers hate to be corrected, so they stay away from the wise.

A woman living in her own strength is a mocker to God and His ways. This is not the position of a truly strong woman. A strong woman knows how to self adjust and find her way back to God. She loves being corrected and looks forward to adjusting her way.

If you are not pleased with your life, then you are opening yourself up to the vulnerability of shame, condemnation and defeat from your enemy. The way to be pleased with your own life, is to believe that God is pleased with you. There is a vast difference between a woman who is just pleased with her life and has no desire to please God, and a woman who pleases God first and then is pleased with herself.

Women who are not pleased with who they are, even if they are pleasing God, will self destruct through condemnation. If you condemn yourself, then it's just a matter of time before everything in your life falls apart.

Pleasing God is the easiest thing you will ever do. There are no complicated steps to pleasing God. There is just one step. Simple. Easy. Anyone can do it. He is so easy to please that you would need guidance on how to mess it up. Here it is: pleasing God is to believe God.

Hebrews 11:6 (NLT) - 6 And it is impossible to please God without faith. Anyone who wants to come to him must believe that God exists and that he rewards those who sincerely seek him.

God is pleased when you activate your heart and mind to believe everything He says. Everything He tells you to do is for your benefit. God wants the best for you, this is why He wants you to believe Him. He is the only one that has your best interest in mind, no strings attached. He has no other reason for your best interest other than He loves you. God loves you whether you please Him or not. He has no other option but to love. John 3:16 shows us this clearly. He loved us when we were sinners, this is why Jesus came: to show us God's unconditional love.

God did not even expect our love for Him to be the way He wants to be pleased. He desires for us to believe Him.

Faith is believing God's Word. Faith comes to you when you hear God's Word. If you don't believe God's Word, then there is no faith. If there is no faith then you cannot possibly, no matter how hard you try, please God.

Romans 10:17 (KJV) - 17 So then faith cometh by hearing, and hearing by the word of God.

You are one step away from being the strongest woman you know. Believe everything God says and vet everything man says. You weaken your God given strong position when you vet what God says and accept what man says.

Offense

Strong women cry, laugh and do mundane tasks. But one thing they know how to do well is not get offended at every little thing that happens to them. My goodness, the amount of women who are walking around offended that they were not included, sought out or acknowledged is astounding. This alone is why so many weak women parade themselves in front of TV news programs spewing their distaste for the way men have been treating them. A strong woman doesn't complain about how they are treated, they let their lifestyle speak for itself.

The ability to walk away from mistreatment is probably one of the most glaring reasons why it is necessary to be a Christian, to be a strong woman. A Christian that is truly following Christ will have the Fruit of the Spirit available for their use. Without this fruit you are left with the shell of human reasoning and temperament to guide you through the treacherous path of land mines placed by Satan against you.

Your enemy hates you. He hates women more than any other creature because she produced the child that defeated him. Jesus destroyed Satan's plan for mankind and God used a woman to deliver Him to the earth (Gen

3:15-16). Women are important to God and hated by Satan. This is a truth that all women should be made aware of.

We should not charge any bad situation in life against God, thinking that God is doing this to teach you a lesson. This is wrong. It is not how God operates. It is clear in the book of Deuteronomy that bad consequences are a result of disobedience to God. Disobedience to God is not initiated by God, it is initiated by us being influenced by the enemy of God. This is exactly what happened in the Garden of Eden. God did not just drive out Adam and Eve and He did not cause their death. Their disobedience did.

Walking closely with God will allow you to stay focused on your purpose for being here. You will put aside silly discussions and feelings of offense. You will not be bothered as much by the words of the crowd. You will be zoomed in on the voice of your Savior. He is your focus.

Closure

A strong woman does not look for closure to move on - she already possesses it. Needing closure, after a hurt or wrongdoing, is a lie that is being fed to society today. Wounded adults wander around life waiting for someone to apologize to them, or for the revenge of someone who did them wrong to be seen. The truth is that Jesus moved on just fine without resolving issues with the people that crucified Him. Why? Because before Jesus committed to being crucified, He knew why He was doing it. This means that no matter what opposition to His purpose He encountered on the way to the cross, He did not seek people's apologies for their actions against Him. If Jesus sought closure, He would have never made it to the cross on time. He would have missed the timing of His purpose. This is what the enemy does to women. He bullies them out of their purpose by building an appetite in them to expect revenge for what has been done to them. This appetite is built by thoughts that they did not deserve to be mistreated, or that someone owes them for all the effort that had been put into their relationship. Whatever missing element you desire to feel important, the enemy will entice you to focus on it. Once he has you focused on that element, you wait for the person you seek to get it from to give it to you before you can move on with life. That is a closure trap.

The enemy uses people to do his dirty work. A good example of this is when he tried to oppose Jesus through the religious folks of His days. Jesus did not succumb to them and you don't have to either. No matter where the opposition for you as a woman comes from, you have to stand strong and stand up for who you were created to be and not lose ground waiting for closure. Closure is not the end of a situation.

The closure is in the beginning. You don't wait for an apology. You walk away after completing your assignment, not after anyone that opposes you apologizes, but when you are finished. When you're in a weakened state you will always be waiting for closure before you can move on. You wait for closure when you do not want to end a relationship or close an issue that causes hurt. You leave the hurt open and you're waiting for an apology or restitution in some way. While you wait, the enemy breathes toxic thoughts into your life. I'm sure that all of us would love to have closure for everything negative that has happened to us, but the reality is that it will never happen all the time.

If you walk with God you will walk with God no matter what someone did to you. You won't get offended at God or family or anyone else for that matter. You will operate like God does. God is not waiting for an end, He makes the end. He is Alpha and Omega. He starts and stops things. You were created in His image and likeness. This means you can start and stop things too. Moving on is normal for a strong woman. Sticking around for closure is a weakened state of being and closure doesn't bring strength. Strength comes from the joy of the Lord (see Nehemiah 8:10).

Position

God says to His people that if they obey His voice He

would make us the head and not the tail.

> *Deuteronomy 28:13 (NLT) - 13 If you listen to these commands of the Lord your God that I am giving you today, and if you carefully obey them, the Lord will make you the head and not the tail, and you will always be on top and never at the bottom.*

This promise is not a gender based promise, neither is it an age based promise. Every person that is a child of God can participate in this and walk in it fully. The level in which you walk in it is between you and God, not you and man. No one can make you close your ears to God. The criteria here for these promises is that you listen and obey God. Not man, but God.

For some reason the enemy has been able to convince women that they don't qualify to be the head of anything. Yet, here we see God making us (all of His children) capable of being the head. The head of what? The head of wherever He's assigned us to be. Wherever we go, we're supposed to walk as if we're the top position not the bottom position. We're to be the leader not the follower. What does this mean? It means we utilize all of ourselves and every gift and ability that God has blessed us with, not wait for someone else to tell us what to do. This is key.

If you walk around life waiting for someone else to lead you to your purpose and destiny, then you will be opening up yourself to destructive missteps that will cause you to fall and fail in what God designed you to do. You will also develop the skill of following but never of leading. To be the head, it means that you also have the vision of direction. God will not make you the head to do nothing. He will make you the head and put the vision of a thing in you. What thing? The thing that pertains to His plans for the place that He's sent you.

When Moses was sent to deliver the children of Israel, he was made the leader of the people by one instruction from God. He did not become the leader gradually moving up the ranks of the tribes of Israel. No, one day he showed up and he was their leader. Because he was their leader, God gave him the plan of deliverance. God didn't give it to the oldest tribal leader, God gave it to Moses.

Wherever God sends you and whatever He asks you to do, He expects you to take ownership of your part. If you're a wife, you should take the head position of being the wife. What does this look like? We will cover this more in a later chapter, but a wife has a job description from God. There is a reason why a woman was created to be wife and if she is to be the head in that position, she needs to know that the reason for this position is from God, not culture. This is so key in being able to take your rightful position in anything you do. Whether you're male or female, you are accountable to God for what you do with what He's asked you to do.

If God has given you an assignment, you must realize that you have already been qualified to do it. God is not a poor judge of character, ability or motive. He knows our innermost thoughts and intents of the heart. He does not have to wonder if we could handle His assignments. He knows we can handle them, He made us with all of the necessary equipment to handle it. So, your ability to do what God has asked you to do should never be in question by you. God is not wondering if you're qualified.

What is the most common thought of women concerning their ability to do what God is asking them to do? From my years of experience in working with women, I have discovered that their number one thought of themselves is that they are always waiting for someone else to validate their decisions. It seems that their own decisions, especially if they are married, are not good enough on their own unless someone (mostly a man) can agree with them or let them know that it's the right thing to do.

The truth is, God would much rather be believed on His own merit than having to be verified by the people you consider to be a voice greater than His.

Does this mean you don't take advice? No! But it does mean you say yes to God first, then you come and work with those in your life. Your yes to God matters greatly. It matters when you say it and if you say it. For example, a woman once said to me that God told her not do something I asked her to do. I quickly accepted her no.

She got highly offended at me for not begging her to stay and work with me. In this case, the person had not really heard from God, they were telling me a lie. They were going by their own selfish ambition. However, I called their bluff. because my policy is, I will never convince someone to do something other than what God has asked them to do. Never!

Growing

A strong woman is not strong once and for all. She continues to grow in the knowledge of God so she can stay strong. She does not remain in a lack of knowledge position. Her strength is in her ability to hear the voice of God and follow it. This is where many people, not just women, feel like they are not sure if it's God, their flesh or the devil. Here is how I deal with this question. My heart is set on doing the absolute will of God. My character, integrity and life guidelines are set on following God's written Word. I have a track record with God for obeying His voice and following it to the best of my ability. With this in mind is how I proceed to do what I think God is asking me to do. If for any reason at all I happen to miss God, He tells me and we move on from there. I don't live a life wondering if it's God with every instruction. That is crippling and destructive to your life. I live in full assurance that I'm a child of God and I know His voice and another I will not follow. God knows that this is my heart's desire and intent. I have given God full permission to correct me in all areas of life. I listen for His voice and correct myself when He reveals it. Sometimes, I've done things for years and then one day God would ask me to stop and do something else. I don't go around crying that I missed God all those years. No, I rejoice that God has given me a new instruction and I'm happy to follow it.

Your growth is directly related to your perspective on God's correction. If you're always condemning yourself if God corrects you, then you will always be bitter at God and think He is never happy with what you do. The devil will come in to reinforce these lies and show you evidence of why this fake news is true.

God is interested in your growth because He is interested in you. The devil is interested in your comfort because He wants you to shrivel up and die.

Comfort or growth, your life choice will determine your lifestyle.

Overall Lifestyle

The overall lifestyle of a strong woman looks like this: Please God by believing and obeying Him and like yourself. That's it.

To get there, you disregard offense. Don't wait for closure. Stand firm in your position as head from God and you grow, grow, grow.

If you can pattern your life to live this way, you will succeed over the enemy every time. You will run and not be weary, you will trust in God and have your strength truly renewed. This is the lifestyle of a strong woman. I leave you with this powerful verse that sums it all up.

Isaiah 40:31 (NLT) -31 But those who trust in the Lord will find new strength. They will soar high on wings like eagles. They will run and not grow weary. They will walk and not faint.

6 THE IDENTITY OF A STRONG WOMAN

In the beginning when God made man and woman, He placed His Words of identity on them. This is what He said:

Genesis 1:26-27 (NLT) - 26 Then God said, "Let us make human beings[a] in our image, to be like us. They will reign over the fish in the sea, the birds in the sky, the livestock, all the wild animals on the earth,[b] and the small animals that scurry along the ground."

27 So God created human beings[c] in his own image. In the image of God he created them; male and female he created them.

After the fall, God did not remove His identity from them. They simply adapted an identity of a sin nature on them because they listened to and obeyed the voice of the original sinner, Satan. In Genesis 3 we see that the consequences of their fall were spoken by God when He manifested His presence to them after they sinned.

One of the things that we did not see God do after He drove Adam and Eve from the Garden, was that He did not reassign their identity to make one bow to the other. How do I know this? Let's look at what God told Noah after the flood.

Genesis 9:1-2 (NLT) - 9 Then God blessed Noah and his sons and told them, "Be fruitful and multiply. Fill the

earth. 2 All the animals of the earth, all the birds of the
sky, all the small animals that scurry along the ground,
and all the fish in the sea will look on you with fear and
terror. I have placed them in your power.

The entire earth's population had been wiped out
except for Noah and his family and the animals that God
put on the ark. God is now starting over with a new family
who He is blessing to keep His covenant with mankind. If
you will note in His blessing, He never once gave Noah or
his sons dominion over their wives. Did He? He put the
fear of all the animals, birds, fish and those creatures that
He made under mankind, but God never once said to
Noah that his wife will be under him. Never, not once.
God's blessing here was also meant for the women. So,
the woman was given the same authority and blessing as
the man. In Genesis 8, God talked about how the earth
was supposed to respond to mankind.

Genesis 8:22 (NLT) - 22 As long as the earth remains,
there will be planting and harvest, cold and heat,
summer and winter, day and night."

The earth was given an assignment to produce for both
men and women. As you can see, everything God made in
the earth was created to be under the authority of man and
woman. He didn't create some things to respond only to
man's voice, so women don't have to get a man every time
she needs to take authority. No, this is not what God
designed and this is not how God wants men to treat
women.

Abraham was a great example in showing a woman's
identity in authority over the affairs of life. Sarah was
having issues with Hagar and her son Ishmael. She came
to Abraham to fix the problem, but here was Abraham's
response.

Genesis 16:5-6 (NLT) - 5 Then Sarai said to Abram,
"This is all your fault! I put my servant into your arms,
but now that she's pregnant she treats me with
contempt. The Lord will show who's wrong—you or
me!"

6 Abram replied, "Look, she is your servant, so deal

with her as you see fit." Then Sarai treated Hagar so
harshly that she finally ran away.

Abraham understood and respected Sarah's position. He did not swoop in as the knight in shining armor to defend her. He defaulted back to her. A strong woman needs a strong man to understand and hold her accountable for what she was given authority to do.

A strong woman's identity is not wrapped up in the identity of another, whether it be father, mother, siblings or husband. It is wrapped up in the position she holds in Christ. She is firm in who she is in Christ and she can back up her decisions with the Word of God. A strong woman's identity is not about her bold personality or her high educational degrees. All of these things are great to have, but they do not make up your identity. They just simply give you tools to use to express who you are.

Your identity was established before the foundations of the world

> *Ephesians 1:4-5 (NLT) - 4 Even before he made the*
> *world, God loved us and chose us in Christ to be holy*
> *and without fault in his eyes. 5 God decided in advance*
> *to adopt us into his own family by bringing us to himself*
> *through Jesus Christ. This is what he wanted to do,*
> *and it gave him great pleasure.*

You were a plan of God before the plan of the world was put in place. As a matter of fact, God created the earth and everything in it for you to enjoy and use. He did not create you for the world; He created the world for you. You get to command things to happen, not just sit back and watch things happen. Joshua commanded the sun to stop so he could finish a fight. The sun obeyed Joshua's command. (see Joshua 10:12-16).

Joshua spoke to God and then spoke to the sun. The sun listened to a human's command and obeyed it. God created you with power and authority. He designed you to have an identity that is clad in the name of Jesus' authority. It is not okay to walk around waiting for someone else to do powerful stuff on your behalf because you're a woman. No, you have been given power and authority because you're a child of God. Here is what's true for you as it is for any man who is also a believer of Jesus:

1 John 4:4 (NLT) - 4 But you belong to God, my dear children. You have already won a victory over those people, because the Spirit who lives in you is greater than the spirit who lives in the world.

The greatness of God should be displayed in all aspects of your life. Not just when you need to show yourself strong or powerful. It should be in all decisions you make in the way you talk about your future, in how you raise your children, and the list goes on and on. You were created with a greatness pack inside you that never runs out of power. It is the Spirit of God that lives in you. You are ready to go when you are born again. There is no time delay in your greatness. However, delays happen because of our lack of knowledge.

I don't know what your knowledge of a woman's identity has been like in your life. But I do hope that so far you can see that there is no difference in God's eyes between a woman and a man when it comes to authority and power over what God has created on this earth.

Let's continue to look at women in the Bible and their positional identities.

Eve

Without Eve, God would have created something that was not good alone. No multiplication of humans could have occurred. There would have just been sperm and no egg. Eggs were needed for multiplication along with a carrying container for the growth. Eve handled that well for humanity. Women still have that capacity and capability today. Incidentally, this is what the enemy uses to get women to once again disobey God. In Exodus 20 we see what God says about human life:

Exodus 20:13(NLT) - 13 "You must not murder.

Yet, the enemy has convinced women that murdering babies is their right as a woman because they have a womb. A woman who lives a lifestyle of pleasing God will have a colossal problem with being the poster child for this evil. A weakened woman supports abortion. This means a woman tainted by the belief system of evil is the one capable of committing such a crime against innocence. But you can change your belief system by building yourself up in the Word of God. As you consider God's ways, you will grow strong and have the right words to say to those who pressure you into this lifestyle.

If you've had an abortion, God is waiting to forgive you. All you need to do is ask God for His forgiveness. You don't have to live with the guilt and shame for the rest of your life. It's your enemy, Satan, that will condemn you into thinking those thoughts of shame.

Eve's identity as the multiplier to mankind's ability to produce life was kept intact after the fall. God did not change the formula of man and woman multiplying. This is still the combination that produces life. A strong woman will recognize this protocol and keep it.

Deborah

Here is a woman who was a double-header. She was a prophet and a judge. She was appointed by God and she fulfilled every aspect of her position. She initiated wars and predicted events.

> *Judges 4:4-5 (NLT) - 4 Deborah, the wife of Lappidoth, was a prophet who was judging Israel at that time. 5 She would sit under the Palm of Deborah, between Ramah and Bethel in the hill country of Ephraim, and the Israelites would go to her for judgment.*

Her actions yielded favorable results for the people she led. She did not waver in her position and it shows that she was a married woman. She was the leader of the country her husband was part of. You can say, in the country perspective, she was his leader. Boy, that would not go over too well with some over achieving religious folks. Somehow in the church environment it has been established that women must bow to men in all positions and men are the only ones allowed to make decisions that affect the masses. Here we have a woman leader who successfully led her army to victory. She also prophesied that a woman would kill the main villain, knowing that it would not be her. She not only led a good war, but she established the identity of another woman. Deborah was sure of who she was. She was not in need of pulling one woman down to attain a high status in society. Weakened women pull other women down. They look for the bad instead of esteeming the good. Strong women will find the strength in other women and help them express their strength to the world.

Esther

Esther had every opportunity to be a cry baby and speak dramatically about her terrible lot in life. She was an orphan who had to live with her male cousin. She had no female influence that we know of, yet, she was born to be a queen. She became queen for a country that was foreign to her. She also became the one ascending voice that triumphed over the murderous plot of a mad man. Esther was beautiful and her beauty was one of the attributes that made up her identity.

> Esther 2:15 (NLT) - 15 Esther was the daughter of Abihail, who was Mordecai's uncle. (Mordecai had adopted his younger cousin Esther.) When it was Esther's turn to go to the king, she accepted the advice of Hegai, the eunuch in charge of the harem. She asked for nothing except what he suggested, and she was admired by everyone who saw her.

Esther's beauty caught the attention of those around her. It also gave her favor with the head eunuch, Hegai. She also accepted the advice of two men, her cousin and Hegai. She did not pretend to have it all together. She was wise and took counsel from those that had the wisdom for what she needed. It's interesting to note in the story of Esther that she never confided in the other girls that were just like her. She was looking for excellence. She needed to look higher than where she was. A strong woman knows who to ask for help and is wise enough to receive counsel. A weakened woman is defensive and thinks that advice is for those who do not know what they're doing. That's so far from the truth. A person that knows what they need to accomplish knows who to ask for help. The more help you can receive the easier the journey and the better the results.

Imagine if Esther did not accept the favor and help of Hegai? She would have rejected God's help to her. God was prepping her for more than queen. She just needed to get to the position of queen so that she could stop the plot of Satan against God's people.

A woman in a weakened state focuses more on what she has to deal with in the moment, than enjoying the journey God is taking her on.

Where is God qualifying you to go? What has He asked you to do? Are you willing to take the first step so He could accomplish the next thing He has planned for the earth? He wants you in on it, but if He constantly has to explain things to you and has to beg you to move forward, it gets a bit tiring, even for God.

Stay focused on listening to God or to those that He has placed around you as advisers. You are strong when you listen to God's instructions and follow them willingly. Reluctance can cause missed opportunity. Esther almost missed the biggest reason why she was there:

> *Esther 4:14 (NLT) - 14 If you keep quiet at a time like this, deliverance and relief for the Jews will arise from some other place, but you and your relatives will die. Who knows if perhaps you were made queen for just such a time as this?"*

Esther's cousin, Mordecai, had to bring a little reality to her. She was now a queen and was adjusting to the lifestyle of the palace. She was safe and comfortable and even though an edict was sent out to kill all of the Jews, of which she was one, she thought that she would be safe. Her cousin reminded her that even she would not be safe, along with her entire family line. Strong women don't just think about themselves they consider those who are coming after them. They are interested in setting up a precedence that can bring life and not perpetuate the curse of evil that has been plaguing their family line. A strong woman puts a stop to evil.

Esther rose up and took action. She made the now famous statement, "If I perish I perish, but I'm going to see the king." (see Esther 4:16). She made a determination to go and see the king, even though it could cause her death if the king did not invite her in. She took bold steps to stop a death sentence for her people. After her speech to the king, the enemy's plans backfired on him. In the end, the people of that country all wanted to be a Jew. The Jews went from being set for hunting to being feared.

> *Esther 8:16-17 (NLT) - 16 The Jews were filled with joy and gladness and were honored everywhere. 17 In every province and city, wherever the king's decree arrived, the Jews rejoiced and had a great celebration and declared a public festival and holiday. And many of the people of the land became Jews themselves, for they feared what the Jews might do to them.*

Esther's bold actions caused joy to fill the Jewish people. They rejoiced at the big win they had over their enemy. This all happened because a woman decided to follow her true identity as a Jew and obey the instructions of her wise counsel to help set her people free. God uses strong women for big jobs. Weakened women are often too scared to do what He's asking them to do. While they are busy questioning their ability to do what God needs them to do, God is looking to see who might take their place. This certainly seems to be what would have happened in Esther's case had she passed up the opportunity. Her cousin was not in agreement with her dropping the ball. You need strong people in your life that will not agree with any weakness you may have, but will pull you up to take action and make strong decisions that could change the future of a whole nation.

Your identity should never be so tightly wrapped around where you came from that you can't let go to see where you need to go. A strong woman grows and changes with God's plans for her life. She can do this even if she's all alone. She is able to take advice and to humble herself before God. A strong woman knows who she is in Christ and keeps learning more about her purchased benefits through the blood of Jesus.

Stay strong and don't let society tell you that you're just one voice, one person and that it does not matter if you do something or not. Everything you do matters for something and for someone. You matter. Stay strong.

SHE IS STRONG

7 A STRONG WOMAN AS WIFE AND MOTHER

I understand that not all women are wives or mothers. In case you are or plan to be, I believe that this information will be helpful to your success as a wife and mother.

For decades Christian women have been plagued with the perfection of the Proverbs 31 woman. It's as if this woman was the ultimate measure of perfection and if you don't attain to her heights you were considered a huge failure and somehow less of a woman. It was escalated to the point where women don't want to hear another thing about this woman and "how great thou art" (well, this is not such a situation). I am going to breakdown Proverbs 31 for you and hopefully from this day forth you will never look at it with condemnation and shame but with expectation and information to use as you choose to build your life. Proverbs 31 is a roadmap of possibilities for women of every era of time. She is the one that probably most closely represents heaven's thoughts about women and her capabilities. Let's see what it's all about.

Proverbs 31 - The Man First

The instructions for this chapter do not start with the qualities of the woman. It starts with the instruction of a woman to her son.

*Proverbs 31:1-3 (NLT) - 31 The sayings of King
Lemuel contain this message, which his mother taught
him. 2 O my son, O son of my womb,   O son of my
vows, 3 do not waste your strength on women,   on
those who ruin kings.*

This mom was advising her son on the type of woman
that he should look for if he wants to be a leader like a
king. So, first of all this type of a woman is the one that
qualifies to help a man that is a leader, he is influential and
behaves like a wise king. In case you're thinking that you
don't want to be married to a king, let me take you to the
New Testament and the book of Revelation:

*Revelation 1:6 (KJV) - 6 And hath made us kings and
priests unto God and his Father; to him be glory and
dominion forever and ever. Amen.*

Right here is where you can find out if the problem is
that you're not good enough or if you're married to a man
that is not qualified to receive from a woman of these
capabilities. The "Proverbs 31" woman described in the
recommendation by this mother, is a picture of what
possibilities exist in a woman.

This mother is sharing wise words with her son to help
him capture the attention of and keep the confidence of
this woman intact during their marriage. She is showing the
potential that exists in a God-fearing woman and the array
of decisions she is capable of making, freeing him up to be
an influence at the highest offices of the land.

Proverbs 31:4-9 is pretty much giving the man advice
on how to be a proper king and leader. He is not someone
that is given to alcohol because he needs to always be in a
state of readiness to give good advice. The husband of this
Proverbs 31 wife needs to be one with wise counsel and
able to be influential in his community. His position is at the
city gates. The city gates are where the elders of the
community would come together to make decisions that
affect everyone that lived there.

Proverbs 31:10-31

The rest of the chapter now deals with the capabilities of a virtuous woman. She is the most qualified helper on the planet for a man. If a man wants to have loneliness removed from him, this helper woman is key. She will not just come and be a companion like a dog, which obeys every command of its master. She will come with her full array of gifts and abilities put in her by God. She is capable of being the biggest help he could possibly find.

> *Proverbs 31:10-12 (NLT) 10 Who can find a virtuous and capable wife? She is more precious than rubies. 11 Her husband can trust her, and she will greatly enrich his life. 12 She brings him good, not harm, all the days of her life.*

As you can see from the verses above, a virtuous woman is to be sought out. She is not someone that just gets plopped down on your lap. She is obviously busy doing what she's great at doing. Looking for a Mr. Right is not her life's ambition. Most stories I hear of how great married couples met happened while each person was very much involved in following an instruction from God. They were all busy doing something. They were not waiting around for someone to just show up. They were living their life. In this case, we see that she is not only pursued, she is also valued and compared to precious stones.

It is interesting that the Bible does not compare a woman to a man. God never did that anywhere He spoke of women. Instead, we see here that a wife is compared to precious rubies. Where did the comparison of men and women come from? The enemy was the one that brought division in the Garden of Eden. In Genesis 3 when God asked Adam and Eve why they ate of the tree, the man blamed the woman and the woman blamed the serpent. Adam was telling God that the help God gave him was an obstacle to him. When in fact, it was the enemy that was the obstacle. God did not change Eve's position after the fall, she was still Adam's helper.

God's view of a helper can be best seen in His

description of Holy Spirit. Jesus told us that He must go so that the Spirit of Truth can come. Holy Spirit was left on this earth as our helper. Does this mean that He is lower than us? Or, does it mean that He does not get a say in what we do? Not at all. Here is how the Bible describes Holy Spirit's relationship to us:

> *John 15:26 (AMPC) - 26 But when the Comforter (Counselor, Helper, Advocate, Intercessor, Strengthener, Standby) comes, Whom I will send to you from the Father, the Spirit of Truth Who comes (proceeds) from the Father, He [Himself] will testify regarding Me.*

The Helper, Holy Spirit, was sent to us to testify of Jesus. He was given to us to help us do what Jesus said we could do. He is the ultimate helper to mankind. When God created mankind He created them in His image. His image was Father, Son, Holy Spirit. In Genesis, Adam declared that a man should leave his mother and father and become one with his wife.

He was expressing a unity in relationship as the unity that exists in the Godhead. God did not create woman from an image apart from Himself. In God there is no sub servant part and a dominant part. God is God. In the same way, human is human. There is not a lesser human and a more dominant, powerful human.

As you will see throughout Proverbs 31, the ability of woman is astounding and limitless. It is the sinful nature of mankind that chooses to limit her potential and ability to give to the earth what the Kingdom of God can offer.

The underutilization of a woman's gifts and abilities is an insult to her Creator.

Your Position on A Woman Like This

I don't know where you stand on such a woman described in Proverbs 31, but I can tell you that she is just an example of the capabilities that God has placed in women. She is not to be despised and shy away from. She should be studied for insight on how she did what she did. The results at the end of the chapter should be your goal.

Your prayer should be for wisdom to get the end result, not to help you not feel condemned for not being like her.

You have been fearfully and wonderfully made. Put together by God skillfully and powerfully. And that was just your human shell. After you are born again as a new creation, you are unstoppable with the power of God that dwells in you. Now all of the human capabilities that you were created with is amped up with Holy Spirit power. Wow! You are unstoppable as a powerful business woman, a mother of children, a wife of a husband, a leader in God's kingdom, a voice in the government, an advocate for the lost. You are designed to renew your mind with the Word of God and to take that renewal to levels that only you could limit.

No matter what you've been taught about being a wife and mother, I suggest you take a look at this Proverbs 31 woman and realize the possibilities that exist in you.

Your Marriage

God does not give intricate details on who does what in a marriage, except to say that there is a man and woman involved. He considers us capable of having a meaningful relationship, where we utilize the gifts in each other. As with Adam and Eve, God did not set a master servant relationship between them.

Wise couples get to know the treasures place by God in their spouse. They should be the first to discover this. This discovery should foster the biggest cheerleading dance you can muster to encourage this great treasure to be shared with the world.

In our house it looks like this: When a new gifting surfaces in one of us (children or adults), we explore how this gift could best serve God's Kingdom and bring glory to Him. We don't tell the person to wait until they're older, or for a more convenient time. If God reveals it to us now, now is when we rejoice in it.

This type of a marriage fosters the best in every person living in your home. A master servant model stifles valuable gifts.

God is not interested in women being "put in their place" by the traditions of men. God expects us to utilize all that He's put in us to conquer the enemy and win territory and hearts for Him. He wants all hands on deck. He is not looking for the work appraisal only of men, He is looking for women to give an account of what they have done with what He's put in them.

A strong woman answers with results to God. A weakened woman has an excuse. Don't let the latter be your position. Take a stand for who you are and who God has created you to be. Have a meeting with the people in your life. Express your heart's desire of what you know that God has asked you to do. Come up with a game plan on how to get things done and go from there. You will be amazed at the strength that will rise up in you from doing such an exercise.

8 GOD NEEDS STRONG WOMEN

When Jesus rose from the dead, His announcement was given by a group of women. They were going to check on His body even though they did not know how they would roll away the stone at the entrance of the tomb.

Mark 16:3 (NLT) - 3 On the way they were asking each other, "Who will roll away the stone for us from the entrance to the tomb?"

These women were going to anoint Jesus' body with spices as was customary for their time. They were still mourning His loss, still hurting from losing Him, but they did not stay in their feelings of sorrow. They got up and took the initiative to treat Jesus' body with the dignity it deserved. But they were in for a big surprise as they arrived at the tomb.

When they got there (see Mark 16) the stone was already rolled away and an angel sat there waiting for them. He greeted them and helped them to send fear away. Then they were given the instructions to go and share the good news of Jesus' resurrection with the disciples. You could say that the first news of Jesus' resurrection was shared first by the women who followed Him, not the men He trained.

The truth is that God needs both men and women for

His kingdom to operate at optimum levels because we each have a unique anointing operating in us that the world needs.

Unfortunately, some women have checked out of the game because of the level of rejection that they have received over the years. What I'm saying to you now is that God needs you to operate in your strength so that His Kingdom can get the glory.

A strong woman seeks after the things of God more than the things that culture expects her to seek. The custom of Jesus' day was that the men would do the big news. Not the women. Jesus changed all of those domineering moves of the enemy and He shared His biggest news with women first.

Anna, The Prophetess

The story of Anna the prophetess who waited in the temple until the dedication of Jesus is amazing. It is a true picture of a strong woman. God made sure that her story was written for us to see.

> Luke 2:36-37 (NLT) - 36 Anna, a prophet, was also there in the Temple. She was the daughter of Phanuel from the tribe of Asher, and she was very old. Her husband died when they had been married only seven years. 37 Then she lived as a widow to the age of eighty-four. She never left the Temple but stayed there day and night, worshiping God with fasting and prayer.

Here is a woman who became a widow after seven years of marriage. She decided not to remarry, but instead remained in God's house to serve God. She rejoiced at the birth of the Messiah. She was useful to God's kingdom because of her work in His house. Her strength was in the waiting to see the Messiah. While she waited she served. Strong women don't let circumstances dictate what they do in life, they define their life by taking actions that can be recorded in history as admirable, and a good example for anyone to follow. She took time to pray, fast and worship God. Women are needed to work in God's house. Anna ministered before the Lord in His house. Strong women serve God and wait for His promises. Anna waited all these years in God's house and saw the greatest gift to mankind, Jesus.

Hannah

There was another strong woman in the Bible that made an impact on the Kingdom of God. For years Hannah was married and never had children. She was distressed by this and kept the desire for children in her heart. Instead of keeping a sorrowful heart, Hannah poured out her heart before God so much so that she was mistaken for being drunk. This deep intercession gave her the answer she was desiring.

> *1 Samuel 1:10-11 (NLT) - 10 Hannah was in deep anguish, crying bitterly as she prayed to the Lord. 11 And she made this vow: "O Lord of Heaven's Armies, if you will look upon my sorrow and answer my prayer and give me a son, then I will give him back to you. He will be yours for his entire lifetime, and as a sign that he has been dedicated to the Lord, his hair will never be cut."*

> *1 Samuel 1:17-18 (NLT) - 17 "In that case," Eli said, "go in peace! May the God of Israel grant the request you have asked of him." 18 "Oh, thank you, sir!" she exclaimed. Then she went back and began to eat again, and she was no longer sad.*

Hannah gave birth to Samuel the next year. As she promised, she took him to the temple to be raised by the priest. This was the customary thing to do in order to train for priesthood. The Bible spoke of Samuel that none of his words ever fell to the ground.

> *1 Samuel 3:19-20 (NLT) - 19 As Samuel grew up, the Lord was with him, and everything Samuel said proved to be reliable. 20 And all Israel, from Dan in the north to Beersheba in the south, knew that Samuel was confirmed as a prophet of the Lord.*

He was the prophet that anointed the first king of Israel, Saul. He anointed David as king. His life was a testimony of a prophet that followed all that God asked him to do. Hannah's intercession was a key to his birth. She was a strong woman who did not allow the circumstances of her life to dictate whether she would receive the desire of her heart. God needs women like Hannah. They may not intercede to be moms but they can pray for God's will to be done on the earth, as it is in heaven. They can carry the intercession for change in their community and homes. God needs strong women who will pray.

Raising Godly Children

A strong woman will raise strong children. Being pregnant and going through the process of having children does not mean that it's the only thing you can do or should do. Choosing to raise children during their childhood years and committing only to that is your free will to choose. There is no model in the Bible where God told child bearing women that this is their only assignment if they are a mother. God created women as the only vessels who can birth the human race to earth. If multiplication of humans will continue to happen on the earth, women will need to give birth to children. Women who give birth are not weak for making the choice to do so, they are fulfilling God's mandate to man to be fruitful and multiply and replenish the earth. There are many things that are replenished in the earth, but only humans can replenish humans. Strong women advocate for the birth of babies, weak women are deceived into killing them. Abortion is a plan of Satan and his world system. Giving birth is a plan of God and His Kingdom system.

If you are a woman that does not want to give birth to children, or have had an issue getting pregnant, it does not mean that you are a weak woman, or less of a woman. It simply means that you have not given birth to children. However, you can still participate in the raising of Godly children. This is something that anyone can participate in should they choose to do so. Why is this important? If the belief system of the Kingdom of God is not taught to children, then the only system that they will learn is that of the world, which is ruled by Satan. Both men and women

SHE IS STRONG

are necessary to participate in this need on the earth. How can you participate in raising godly children? There are children all over the world that are orphans, looking for someone to care for them. There are Christian organizations that have taken on this challenge and are working hard to help children realize their God given potential and purpose for being on earth.

In my personal life, even though I have children of my own, I run an orphanage located in Guyana, South America. My mom and dad started Bless The Children Home in 2008. They were both living in the US and getting ready to retire. God gave my mom a dream that changed our lives forever. She saw children being raised in a home that was surrounded by love and peace. She saw children learning about who they are and why they are here on earth. Since then, we have had many children come and go through our orphanage. Today, I am the President of that organization and am responsible for the raising of many children, more that I could ever give birth to in a lifetime. Since I've taken over the leadership of this mission, I've expanded our help of these children to their adulthood. After they turn 18, they are expected by the governmental system to now live on their own. Unfortunately, some of them are not prepared simply because they got a late start at stability in life. Some of them are not caught up like their peers in school, or may have not yet overcome the trauma that sent them to us in the first place. So I am not too keen on sending them off at 18. Instead, I've developed a plan that allows them to come to the US and go to Bible School. Our first child to participate in this program started in January of 2019. Months later she has grown so much. Her knowledge of God has grown exponentially. Her experience in life skills has leaped from theory to practical and her love for God and who she is in Christ has been captured so potently that no amount of telling her about these things would have accomplished this. But, giving her the opportunity and supporting her exploration of this God given life is my role now. I am her mother yet I never adopted her, nor gave birth to her.

She is an intercessor in God's Kingdom. She

participates in praying for the nations at her school. She is holding up in prayers the staff and children that now reside in the home she came from. She prays for me.

I am raising her to be a strong woman of God, yet I never gave birth to her. Women of God, our young ladies and young men need us. Look around you, what family is struggling to raise their children? Do you have neighbors that don't take their kids to church? Have you ever considered offering to take them yourself to church? Think outside of your own family, and reach beyond. This is how we will take more territory for the Kingdom of God, other than what was born to us. We have to reach out to the generations of the future and rescue them from being conformed to the systems of the world. Help them get transformed. God needs strong women to stand up and raise godly children all over the world.

Single Women

What if your situation is different and you have no desire to be a wife or a mother, even for other people's children? What can you offer to the Kingdom of God? Paul says it best when he wrote about singleness and marriage.

1 Corinthians 7:7-9 (NLT) - 7 But I wish everyone were single, just as I am. Yet each person has a special gift from God, of one kind or another.

8 So I say to those who aren't married and to widows— it's better to stay unmarried, just as I am. 9 But if they can't control themselves, they should go ahead and marry. It's better to marry than to burn with lust.

If you can handle being single, then do it. The purpose for doing this though would be to use your time, resources and energies to do things for the Kingdom of God that married people are not able to do because of time needed for relationship. A strong single woman should be decisive on her calling from God and should fulfill it with passion and commitment. Don't stay single but yet bemoan the fact that you are not married. Don't feel guilty that you never found "the right one". Don't condemn yourself like that. Make good use of the time your singleness affords you.

God needs you. Ask Him to show you what to do and do it well. Don't waver, or do it with the thought that someday you won't have to do this anymore. Do it with joy and let God reward you for your work in His Kingdom.

Bold, Fearless Women

In my traveling and teaching I find women who desperately want to be bold and fearless. They hear me speak and they want to speak like I do. So, they would ask me how I could be so bold and speak with such authority and confidence. My response is always the same, I express who God created me to be. I deliver the messages God has put in me through the personality and gifts and abilities He's blessed me with. I use up all of my gifting and talents when I do something for God. I pull from everything I know. His anointing is His empowerment over me while I use those gifts. I activate that anointing while I minister. The way I do that is to step out by faith and when I speak or pray for people, results follow. I activate the anointing in me by using my free will to choose to cooperate with Holy Spirit. I listen for His voice and obey His instructions.

Other's fast and pray and wait and pace and do other things, but that's them. I'm a fast paced girl and I like that God made me this way. He uses me in quick things. This is the strength God has blessed me with, and I walk strong in it. A strong woman maximizes the anointing of God to benefit others.

If you want to benefit others with your life, you must walk in fearless boldness that utilizes the Spirit of God of love, power and a sound mind. Paul told young Timothy this and it applies to women as well:

> 2 Timothy 1:7 (KJV) - 7 For God hath not given us the spirit of fear; but of power, and of love, and of a sound mind.

What do you want God to do with your life? What is it that you are frustrated about and seem to think that everyone else is getting their "it" and you're not? The answer may be in one decision you need to make. I've found that strong women make decisions independent of life's circumstances because she is not afraid. She goes for what she knows God wants her to do. She does not compete with the lady next to her, she has enough of the Spirit of God in her to help others along the way.

Have you been holding back your dreams and afraid to be you? I am encouraging you to ask God consistently what He wants you to do next. Don't assume what you should do next. Many women that are married with children always make plans based on the age of their kids and the jobs of their husbands. They are always in a position of waiting. They think in terms of as soon as my last child leaves home I will be able to do so and so. Or, as soon as my husband finds a job in such and such a place I will finally be able to do . . . That mentality causes you to lose a little bit of who you are everyday. Then, 18 years later you think it's too late or it's too hard to gain it all back. But it's not!

If you find yourself in this position, don't dismay. You can pick up where you left off anytime. Your actions in God's kingdom are run by faith. Faith is the now feature of your Christianity. It is always in the present. So by faith you can believe God to do the things that you might have missed doing in your years of raising kids or following and helping your husband in his career.

At the writing of this book, my husband and I will soon be celebrating 22 years of marriage. I entered marriage with an MBA (Masters of Business Administration) degree. I've worked in several industries and for many types of bosses. I've also helped my husband fulfill the desires God put in his heart to fulfill. I mothered two children, Gabriel (16) and Josiah (7). During all of these years of marriage and motherhood, not once did I ever think that what I ever wanted to do could wait until my kids were older or until my husband's goals were met. Not even once did I think this way. Unfortunately, in some cultures married women with children would be considered selfish if she expressed her desire to advance her education or career. She may be frowned upon and considered to be a bad mom or wife for leaving her family to pursue her dreams, but that is following culture's standards not my heavenly Father's design for me. I know better and so I am required to do better. One of my life's statements is, "To whom much is given much is required" (see Luke 12:48).

As it stands now, my husband is the lead pastor of a local church, I am the executive pastor with him. I am also the president of Bless The Children Home Orphanage located in Guyana, South America and the CEO of Fiona Inc. a life coaching company started in 2006 at the direction of Holy Spirit. In all of these positions and roles that I've fulfilled over the years, I have helped many people besides my family. My children are well adjusted to life and can socially interact with any age group or people groups. They can make decisions for themselves and still know how to cuddle up to mom for comfort and support. My seven year old knows that he can come to me and say, "Mom I'm angry at you" and then proceed to tell me what his plight might be with me for the day. I don't get offended when he does this because I know I'd rather him tell me than keep it bottled up inside. We don't have outbursts of pent up frustration in our home because everyone can speak what they need to speak without threats, pouting or accusations of personal insults. We didn't get there overnight, but we got there quickly. How? Because both my husband and I can listen to the voice of Holy Spirit and be corrected as we need to be along life's pathway. If we don't think we should be corrected, how could we model correction for our children? Our children know that correction is necessary and have seen the positive results of correcting our steps along the way. We model these things in our home. No one sits around waiting for the right moment to do something. The only time in our home where time stood still was when we cared for my parents who were living with us and going through cancer treatments. Time seemed to have stood still in those months. But we made it through as a family. I spent more time with my parents that year than with my kids. I was missed but not resented. When my parents died within months of each other, my family was able to put ourselves back together quickly and rejoice for their new home in heaven, and keep living the life God wants us to have here on earth.

These strong moves in my life did not happen overnight.

It did not happen by chance, it happened because I spoke up when necessary and stayed quiet when needed. When my husband and I first got married I would point out things on the road as he was driving (I think we all do this at some point in our life). At first my husband would be a bit uptight about the whole thing, but who wouldn't be right? But, I made this statement to him and we have kept this as part of our marriage for every area since. I said to him that I am not afraid of his anger at my correction because I would never want to walk into the emergency room one day and tell him that I saw the vehicle coming, but didn't want to tell him because he would get angry. "I'm not afraid of your anger" is probably one of the most profound statements I've ever made in my marriage. The truth is my husband rarely ever got angry about anything. He is the most even keel person you'll ever meet. However, when he had an opinion of something, he was strong in it. This is where I would have to stand up if I saw a different perspective. Because I was willing to not be afraid of anger, I was able to foster an environment in our home where none of us are afraid to say what we need to say. The person receiving the words has to grow in their reception of things not us change our pointing out of things.

The way I live my life may be nothing compared to how you would like to live your life. And that's okay. The key is that you need to choose how you want to live your life now. Don't wait for the "right" time. The right time is always now. Tomorrow will have its own assignments, start taking steps to do what God wants you to do now. Don't wait for your husband or children to do it first. Do it when God shows it to you.

I'm about to start my doctoral program in business administration. Do I have time for this? In the natural, I could say I don't, but I am confident that this is the right thing for me to do. Why? Because it was an instruction from God. When He gives me an instruction I follow it as quickly as I can. I feel like I've missed this instruction before, so when He brought it back to me I quickly accepted. When I accept an assignment from God, I don't ask permission from my family to do it. That's how we've designed our home. We are all free to accept God's request of us apart from checking in with each other. It's how God started Jesus' journey on earth. Mary was asked to carry Jesus without any input from Joseph (see Luke 1). Then, what we do is we collaborate on how we can help each other accomplish the assignments God has given to us.

God will work in your life based on the protocol you've set up in your home. Whether you're married with kids or single, you have a protocol of your household that can either let God be free to give you assignments or hold things back until you feel like you're able to handle it. God will never break your will to make you do His will. He is not a dictator He's God.

As you can imagine, I consider myself a strong woman. I don't wear this title because I think I know everything and am strong in every area of life. I am strong because I strengthen weak areas when they're pointed out to me. I work on being better even in the areas I'm already strong in. I always make myself available and ready to do whatever God needs done on this earth. If He needs it and thinks I'm the gal for the job, I agree with Him and don't hesitate to start stepping in that direction.

Sometimes it means waking up at 3 or 4 am to pray so that I can fit this time with God into my day before everyone is up and needs my help. Sometimes it means that my husband gets our son ready for school while I sleep in because I was up at wee hours of the morning praying or writing. I do not feel guilty about having help in my home to do what needs to be done. I know why I'm here and what God wants me to do while I'm here. In other words, I know my purpose.

Do you know your purpose? Psalm 139 talks about how God has written a book about our life before we were even born. In this book is His perfect will for our life. Ask Him to reveal its content to you and share your desire to walk in it. Once He's revealed any part of it with you, do it. Don't wait for the rest, do what He reveals and more will be given to you.

When I started my business I called it Fiona Inc.

because I didn't know what the business would be. I had no idea what God wanted me to do in this business, but I set it up anyway. A few months later, my first client came and asked for me to mentor them. God had asked them to talk to me months earlier (the month I setup the business) but they thought I was too busy and never did. God reminded them of it and that's when they approached me for my help. From that time until now, some of the programs I designed for this one client have been the same programs that have worked for men and women around the world.

Who have you dreamed of always helping? Did you know that you are an amazing creation of God? When He created you strength was already part of your DNA. The circumstances of life and culture of the world system is what weakens you. This means that you can gain strength quickly once you've made up your mind to stand up and do what God has asked you to do.

Follow His instructions one step at a time. Ask Him to remind you of what He may have told you years ago but you never took steps to get it done. It's what I did recently, and that's when He reminded me of my doctoral degree. Since I've said yes to doing the degree, He has revealed to me a little bit of the why He needs me to do it.

What if I had the mentality that I can't do these big things now, I'm a mom and a wife and my first priority is to my family? I would miss out on God's agenda being my first priority. Our family was also given to us by God, He won't give us competition. If your family and God are in competition with each other, someone is out of place and I can guarantee you it's not God. Start turning your life boat around little by little, and put God in the proper place, then watch and see if every other decision will not make sense and work better for you.

God needs you that's why He created you. Make sure that you've doing all that He needs you to do. If you are already on that track, then rejoice in it and help other people get there. If you find that you are not even close to being on track, don't fret, take one step at a time. Go in your prayer closet and ask God to reveal to you His instructions because you're listening. Listen and obey. That's how you build your strength in your purpose. No one else can do this for you. You have been designed to fulfill God's plan for your life by your own free will.

9 MAINTAINING YOUR STRENGTH

Strength is not a permanent position. It requires the right nurture to maintain its potency. There are a few factors that can contribute to weakness in any area of life, and when those factors are activated for a long period of time, strength can disappear and weakness moves in like a thief in the night. Strength is like a muscle, the more you use it the stronger it gets. With inactivity muscles weaken.

My mom was hospitalized for two months towards the end of her life. The day she got to the hospital she walked to her bed. When she left the hospital she was taken out by a wheelchair to a rehabilitation facility to build her muscle strength back up. What happened in two months that made her go from actively mobile to practically paralyzed? Inactivity. She laid in bed more than she walked around. Her muscles became less and less active. Eventually, she stayed in bed because it was easier than getting up. It was more comfortable for her. No one, including her, realized what this inactivity was doing to her leg muscles. Until one day, we were helping her out of bed and her knees began to buckle. We had never seen anything like it. It was painful for her to stand. She almost fell to the ground. Two months is all it took for this very active woman to lose the use of her legs. Strength is relative to the activity we choose to embrace. My mom's strength left her legs because of inactivity.

What areas of your life do you feel like you've been inactive in and may have lost all strength? Do you feel depressed? Do you feel joyless, hopeless or lost for purpose? Were you strong once, then one day you start wondering who you were and why you could not make one simple decision without second guessing yourself. Maybe you have always been weak in decision making, but you don't have to be. Whatever the reason, the past is the past and you are here now and have been given permission by heaven to make decisions for your own life.

God shows us this in Deuteronomy.

Deuteronomy 30:19 (NLT) - 19 "Today I have given you the choice between life and death, between blessings and curses. Now I call on heaven and earth to witness the choice you make. Oh, that you would choose life, so that you and your descendants might live!

God's choice is always that you choose life. What does that look like? It looks like satisfaction, fresh air, fulfillment, completion, reward and joy. These are just a few of the results that are ignited when you make life choices. If you have a problem making choices though, you may feel stifled, suffocated or downright sick to the stomach for even having to make a choice. It doesn't matter what the choice was. Just the fact that you made a choice by yourself without anyone's input could be scary for someone who has never truly made decisions on their own. If this is your situation, you want to know that your decisions are not void of God's presence. He said that He has set before you life and death. This means that He is there with you. Holy Spirit is your helper to lead and guide you into all truth. Learning how to hear the voice of God and utilizing His help in matters of your life is key to being a strong woman and making sound decisions.

John 16:13 (NLT) - 13 When the Spirit of truth comes, he will guide you into all truth. He will not speak on his own but will tell you what he has heard. He will tell you about the future.

To be truly strong in making decisions and standing in them, you must utilize the full power of God in your life. To have access to this full power, we've been given the opportunity to receive Holy Spirit with the evidence of speaking in tongues. I don't know your thoughts on this or your knowledge of it, but it is a vital key to standing strong as a person, even more a woman of God. I say more for a woman of God not because women are weaker, but because women are being attacked more and more to stay dormant, silent and irrelevant. They are locked out of decisions that could change the world. It's time for the women in the Body of Christ to rise up and take their strong positions in all walks of life. In politics, church leadership, business, communication, education, finances and all types of industries. God wants both men and women in those places. Psalms talks about the great host of women who publish the good news.

> Psalm 68:11 (AMPC) - 11 The Lord gives the word [of power]; the women who bear and publish [the news] are a great host.

Today, you should want to be part of the great host of women who publish the Word of power that God gives. What word or instruction of power has God asked you to share with the world? Share it, act on it, multiply it through those around you.

There is a saying that if you teach something you will learn it faster. I want to encourage you today to teach your strength to your peers and the next generation around you. The Bible is full of scriptures that show God asking the Israelites to pass lessons down to their children and children's children.

> Deuteronomy 4:9 (AMPC) 9 Only take heed, and guard your life diligently, lest you forget the things which your eyes have seen and lest they depart from your [mind and] heart all the days of your life. Teach them to your children and your children's children—

If you can think generationally you are thinking in the frequency of God's thoughts. He does not think of our time, He is thinking of ages to come. From the beginning of time until now many generations have walked this earth. Among them were both strong and weak women. In the Word of God we see how strong women like Mary, Elizabeth, and Sarah followed God's plans and instructions while weak women like Jezebel and Delilah manipulated their way into situations. God's power in you is so strong and powerful that manipulation will be seen for the evil system that it is. Delilah and Jezebel were two manipulators who did not finish well. Jezebel's body was lapped up by dogs while Delilah lost the love of one of the strongest men alive. Both women could have influenced the men in their life and even their country for God, instead they choose their own power and control through manipulation.

The Will of Heaven

In the prayer model that Jesus shared with the disciples at their request there is a line that stands out to me. It is something I explain to women when they are not sure if they are supposed to do something or not.

> *Matthew 6:10 (AMPC) - 10 Your kingdom come, Your will be done on earth as it is in heaven.*

Jesus told the disciples to pray that God's will be done on earth as His will is in heaven. With this in mind, I want you to examine the areas of your life that you have questions concerning the will of God and ask yourself these questions: Would God be against me doing this in heaven? Does God have different jobs for men and women in heaven? Will I get to be a leader in heaven?

To give you an idea of what God would allow in heaven, take a look at what Jesus allowed on earth. When it came to women, Jesus accepted women's gifts of worship to Him (Luke 7:37). He spoke to women who were thirsty and told them they could drink from His living water and they did (John 4). He healed women publicly that society had condemned to solitude because of their condition (Matt 9:20). His ministry was supported by women, who traveled with Him and His disciples during ministry (Luke 8). He was friends with Mary, Martha and their brother, Lazarus (John 11). Jesus valued women and their input into society and His life. He performed His first miracle at the wedding feast at the request of His mother (John 2).

We see in the way Jesus treated women that He did not hold back anything that God made available to mankind from women. He healed them, He added them to His ministry team, He taught them and did not expect them to just prepare meals for Him (Mary and Martha's story), and He accepted their suggestions to help others (His Mother at the wedding). Jesus respected women and their callings. He never tried to put a woman in "her place" or society's box. Women were free in Jesus' presence.

It is the same with Heaven's will. Jesus said that He did not do anything He didn't see His Father do (John 8:28), and Jesus never sinned. This proves that it is not sinful or wrong for a woman to hold any position in God's Kingdom that He has called her to. Nor is it sinful for her to make decisions to do God's will without the permission from someone else in her life. Women have the same rights and opportunities as men according to heaven's will. Jesus came to earth to realign the earth with the will of heaven concerning our authority and rights to the Father. Here is what Galatians says about this truth:

Galatians 3:28 (NLT) - 28 There is no longer Jew or Gentile, slave or free, male and female. For you are all one in Christ Jesus.

Every woman can walk in the freedom that Jesus purchased for them. They don't have to be watching from the sidelines anymore, waiting for a chance to be treated equally. The world will keep fighting that battle until the end of time. In the Kingdom of God, that battle has already been fought and won by Jesus for all women who will receive His free gift of Salvation.

So, what's your choice today? Strong woman or struggling woman?

As for God, He sees nothing else but strength in your future.

Philippians 4:13 (NLT) - 13 For I can do everything through Christ, who gives me strength.

FIONA PYSZKA

Check out other books from Fiona

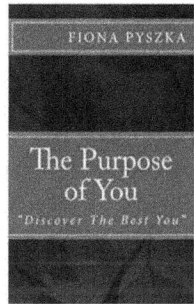

Available on amazon

fionainc.com

Write to:
Fiona Inc.
P O Box 164, Palmyra PA 17078

ABOUT THE AUTHOR

Fiona Pyszka is an International Speaker, Personal Development Coach, Life Motivator, Strategist and Author of seven books including her personal best seller: Fearless. She is also the CEO of both Fiona Inc. and Bless The Children Home Orphanage in Guyana. Fiona Inc. is a company dedicated to helping people discover and live their purpose by providing personal coaching development and tools for people of all ages and backgrounds.

She is known for her strategic solutions, for teaching you how to live out your purpose and identity without fear or failure. Her books reinforce her ability to bring to life and develop an individual's purpose, confidence, identity, courage and relational skills. Fiona's most powerful and influential messages address Fear, Purpose and Strategy.

Raised a preacher's kid in Guyana, South America, Fiona knows what it is like to pursue and fulfill your purpose. She has a BA from Lee University, an MBA from Regent University, is an ordained minister, an Executive Pastor and has worked in management in a number of industries and Fortune 500 companies.

Fiona's most powerful and influential messages address Fear, Purpose and Strategy.

Fear

Fear controls your decisions and your future. But you are more powerful than fear. Learn how to conquer what has held you back and activate the power to move forward with who you were created to be.

Purpose/Vision

Your future deserves your attention. Discovering who you are propels your future. Each of us has positions to fulfill and authority that accompanies each of those positions. Stand up and take your place. The world is waiting for what you have to offer.

Strategy

Many believe that they must wait to fail in order for success to begin. Nonsense! Failure is not the required path for a successful life. You have a story; you are qualified to win; you can avoid traps and you can speak success into your life. Strategies to win in everything you do are right around the corner.

If you would like to schedule Fiona at your next event, contact us at:

Fiona Inc.
P O Box 164
Palmyra, PA 17078

Or Visit: fionainc.com

www.ingramcontent.com/pod-product-compliance
Lightning Source LLC
Chambersburg PA
CBHW072007060426
42446CB00042B/2231